The Ghetto Grocer

I0412908

50 True Tales of Food Market Misadventure

Dust Cover

James LaFond has worked in, managed and consulted for supermarkets in the Baltimore Area since 1981. In The Ghetto Grocer he addresses the following issues in his politically incorrect style:

What food handling standards are observed in supermarkets?

What does 'clean' mean to a supermarket manager?

How might your fresh meat be mishandled?

How does shoplifting impact the food retailer and you?

What types of crimes occur in supermarkets?

How exactly are your tax dollars spent by the starving oppressed who receive WIC vouchers, EBT cash, and food credit?

What is it like to do some of the worst jobs in a food store, and what kind of people work where your food is prepared and displayed for purchase and consumption?

And if the End Time comes, what is going to be left on the supermarket shelves on Day Three?

The Ghetto Grocer

The Ghetto Grocer

Dedicated to the men and women of retail food,
may you reach retirement doing something else

Contents

Preface

I have no desire to implicate any former coworker or employee in anyway, and have therefore changed the names of all establishments and all persons named in this memoir of a working life spent among people who all wished to be elsewhere. I thank them all, each and every one of them, for providing me with priceless insights into the collective anguished mind of the servile class and the equally—though differently—tortured minds of their immediate masters.

It is my thought, as I consider these tales written over the past few years that it is about time that the men and women of retail and their alternately silver-spooned, industrious, and corporately robotic task-masters deserve the credit they are due for feeding this ballooning nation of fat lazy fucks!

Based on the girth of our population the humble grocery clerk is product enough to earn the praise of many a supply master tasked with feeding the ravenous armies of old.

-James LaFond, Monday, October 13, 2014

The Last Can of Food on Earth: Chef LaFond's Post-Apocalyptic Kitchen

© 2012 James LaFond

It will be barely a month before the ghosts of the Mayan astronomers begin hurling comets at us. In that case, it is a about time that I finally test my oldest surviving retail food ration. Now, when one thinks of eating after the coming apocalypse, visions such as Mel Gibson grubbing around in a can of dog food while his pet dog whines in the background, or of Denzel Washington roasting an irradiated cat in an abandoned farmhouse, come to mind.

What will it really be like?

The Ghetto Grocer as Archaeologist

As a grocer for these past three decades I have gained some renown as an archaeologist of sorts. My first foray into store resets was in 1980, when, as a grocery clerk, I reset the granola bar section to make way for new arrivals. As I was cleaning and adjusting the shelf backing I discovered a grim morsel, a discontinued type of granola bar from the mid 1970s. A raw seed in the mix had sprouted, and a small tree was busting through the cardboard box, reaching for the florescent lights above. After tossing this rare find, and being stricken with guilt for dashing the hopes of that overoptimistic seedling, I decided to save the next ancient discovery I made.

My next chance was the winter of 1984 when chunky soups came out, and we had to make room. During the course of the canned soup set I discovered a can of Campbell's Cream of Onion condensed soup. It had been produced in 1978 and had gone out-of-date in December 1981. I still have this can. It has served as a bookend/science experiment ever since. Fortunately, a year ago, just in time for my preparations for the coming apocalypse, my X returned it to me—why, I have no idea.

The dates on these old solidly built cans were 4 years. An expiration date on a shelf-stable grocery item is not supposed to be when something goes bad, just a way for the manufacturer to be able to lay the blame on the retailer if the thing does morphs into a lycanthrope under a winter moon and attacks grandma in her pantry. The new zip-top cans only come with 24 to 18 months on them. Everything else on the dry shelves is pretty much guaranteed for a year to 6 months. Interestingly enough pasta has about the longest declared shelf-life.

I am no stranger to old canned goods. In the late 1970s, when I made $60 per week, I shopped at the military surplus store. I routinely dined on such Korean War vintage delicacies as beef with gravy [very stringy], beans and franks, and chocolate nut roll; the later being a bit dry after 27 years in a can. If you have not stocked up for the End of Days you might want to know that supermarkets rely on 2 to 7 shipments weekly. That means when a disaster hits and everyone in the area descends on them, they have from 2 to 3.5 days worth of what people want on hand.

Assuming, that years from now, you are still sitting on a stash of canned goods, ducking into your hidey hole to munch away as the cannibal caravan scours the neighborhood, what are the chances that it will still be any good?

The Ghetto Grocer

I sit wondering the same thing, as I gaze suspiciously at this little morsel of milk, wheat and onion, hermetically sealed on some long-retired canning machine in New Jersey. Setting aside the advisability of eating something flavored by balding chemists in New Jersey, would this really be edible? If so, would it be palatable?

According to everyone I know I am not to be trusted where palatability is concerned.

...My roommate once left a fast food burger in the lettuce crisper for five days. I tried microwaving it. The thing just became more desiccated, impossible to cut. You see, I can't get my mouth around a sandwich due to an old boxing injury. I was looking forward to dining on some emaciated Brazilian cow, and was not to be denied. I had purchased a pouch of out-of-date black beans and 'sauce' and decided to use that as a softening agent. After 3 more minutes in the countertop nuke I had a steaming repast in my hands. I sat down to watch the Geek Chanel and barely had to saw with my butter knife! The roll had been marginally reconstituted, kind of like a biscuit. The 'beef' did yield to my attempts at mastication. The black beans and 'sauce' went down easily enough. I would have to say however, that the microwave had not done the tomato and lettuce justice…

Today, in our time of plenty, you might not want to share my version of dinner, living as I do on $15 of food per week. Ten years into the End of Days, however, you might just think I'm the next best thing to Paula Dean, and invite me in to garnish your potted meat food product stew.

Now, to the can in question: Cream of Onion condensed soup is no longer a shelf item, and is only produced as a food service item. A can should be good so long as no air gets in. This will cause a growth of bacteria and a swelling of the can. I am sorry to say, that sometime early this week, my can began to swell—the long arm of the extinct astronomers being longer then even I thought. So I will not be eating this stuff. However, in the name of culinary science I will test the contents in the confines of my roommate's kitchen—which is a lab of sorts.

So, having declared this item unsafe to eat and hazardous to store after 34 years, we have established a base-line shelf-life of 33 years for an old school canned good with a 4 year shelf life, eight times the declared shelf-life. For modern canned goods reduce this to 6-times the shelf-life, and, for zip-tops, 3 times. This results in a life-span of 6 to 12 years for the modern canned good. Now, my work as a scientist done, I advance to my role as a doctor of culinary forensics...

...Here it goes. Any moment now I shall amble downstairs, simulating my emergence from a hiding place after the passage of the cannibal caravan [or Zombie horde, whichever you prefer] and crack open, The Last Can of Food on Earth!

I sit now with the tin corpse before me, and is not smelling too good. There was a slight, barely perceptible, swelling of the can—first stage. When I punctured the top with the can opener a milky foam emerged with a hiss; a pathetic geyser about two millimeters in height. This was enough to quash any thought of taking an experimental taste.

The contents were a thick yellowish paste that looked very much like sweetened condensed milk in a can. After scooping the can-shaped mass into the trashcan I had every intention of retaining the can as a bookend, if only a flyweight guardian of my evangelic religious comics collected at ghetto bus stops. The can did have a vestigial onion smell, like that onion rack I cleaned out twenty years ago in a city supermarket. The bags of onions had gone so long without being rotated that those on the bottom were reduced to brown ooze seeping from their net bags.

As I scrubbed I noticed the smell growing worse—**abort, abort; danger of contamination!** There was also a brown film, like an oxidized gruel, covering the interior of the can. Extreme janitor that I am, I remained fully confident that I could banish this muck, but at what cost?

That is right antique Americana geeks: to save the can I must kill the label. And what is a trophy can without its label?

Out he goes, after 34 years of service, discarded.

Now, for the sake of our post apocalyptic extrapolation, we should close this out with a mental image, of you and I watching the rearguard of the cannibal caravan prowling off into the sunset. The realization that our last can, our last edible vestige of pre-apocalyptic life, had been rendered inedible must dampen our mood—"Wait, was that a cat I saw dart behind the burnt out conversion van on the lawn? Get the wrist rocket! I'll get the soy sauce. That couldn't have gone bad; it was made in Japan."

Toxic Toddler Planet: Hydration Profiteering and the Stupidest Ape in the Galaxy

© 2013 James LaFond

Tapped

Yesterday I viewed Tapped, by Atlas Films, a documentary on bottled water politics. Unlike most of the documentaries I view it was pretty main stream, made by people who believe that Uncle Sam is not a pedophile…

The documentary has the usual litany of lying obfuscating corporate spokesdroids, pie-in-the-sky activists, really smart scientists, really stupid government regulators, inconsolable victims of corporate greed and toxic dumping…all of the untouchable bad guys and ineffectual good guys that have made news programs such as 60 Minutes good informative soul-crushing entertainment since I was a little brat.

I recommend this film for anybody and everybody. Let me give you my personal experience with the subject in hopes of adding some perspective.

Note: I will make no effort to spell check the names of major corporations. They are not worth the wear and tear on my finger joints.

Nasty, Brutish and Never-ending

I have worked my entire adult life in retail food. In 1981 the bottled water section contained a case pack worth of distilled water for car batteries and home medical equipment, and a case pack worth of imported sparkling water in a glass bottle. That is not even a half of a lineal foot in the beverage aisle. Today, I would never set a store with less than 32 lineal feet of shelving allocated for water. This is minimal and would need to be supplemented with pallet displays. We buy these pallets of 72 24-pack cases a tractor trailer at a time.

One pallet of water is a ton-and-a-half of stuff [on an 80-lb wooden frame pallet that some guy that was too short to play high school basketball has to stack 7 feet high] you need to process that only makes you about $40. By the time you're done paying the chain-smoking receiver to drag it off the truck, the alcoholic clerk to display it, the domestically abused cashier to ring it up, and the Downs' Syndrome kid to put it in someone's trunk, there is not a lot of rape-and-pillage room for the manager and owner—then there is the 50K a month utility bill, the million dollar a year rent, the 50K a year in slip-and-fall settlements...The bottom line is food retailers work on a .5% to 2% profit before equipment and remodeling purchases. They just provide local jobs. The money is made by the manufacturer.

In the early 1990s we grocery clerks joked about what kind of idiot would buy bottled water. Now we are those idiots; without a water fountain to drink from, two old to drink sodas and milk, in too much of a hurry to sip coffee like some hung-over construction worker, and too poor to drink juice smoothies except on pay day...

The film makers of Tapped focus on Nestle [the main force in bottled water politics], Pepsi and Coke, who each have numerous brands of bottled water.

The first major issue is that these companies pump municipal water—purified with tax dollars—for free, and then compete against that water supply and sell the bottled version back to us at astronomical profits, and the bottles end up polluting that same water supply.

The second major issue is the fact that the manufacture of the PET bottles poisons people near the production facilities, that drinking from the bottles poisons the giant toddler that is the modern person as they walk around sucking on them, and that the discarding of these bottles is poisoning the oceans.

Where this film is incomplete is in their targeting of the soft drink companies. Coke and Pepsi use far more water in bottling their sodas than in bottling water, and earn even larger profits. Also, if the water in these bottles can leach out the benzenes and other chemicals that cause a slew of health issues, what do you think that Coca Cola does? My father-in-law used Coke to remove road tar from the tires of his family car.

In 2006 I took a position as the general manager of an independent food market after 25 years as a grunt for various independent and corporate outfits. This was a four year gig to get my youngest son through college before I dropped back out of the economy. I had been setting up stores for most of those two and a half decades and knew going in that soda was the new 'milk'.

Supermarkets have been traditionally set up so that milk and bread, the two staples of the traditional American diet, were farthest from the front door. This would require the shopper to pass by everything that actually makes a profit for the market, and hopefully buy some of it. Items like milk and bread that are staples are not profitable for the retailer, as they are the object of intense competition. Sooner rather than later some retail food honcho will decide to give the stuff away to take customers away from the competition, and then everybody is doing it. Such items are called 'loss leaders'.

The last two stores I set with soft drinks back with, or even behind, the milk. This is not because sodas sell more than milk. They don't, though they are closing in. This is done because, while milk is a very low profit item, sodas are a zero profit item! You see, milk is milk. But Coke is Coke, not Pepsi, and certainly not Randy Andy Pop. Now that the modern adult toddler and its brood are thoroughly addicted to sweetened carbonated beverages marketed for a century as brand-loyalty-based delicacies, 'loss leader' status for these products has put the two big soda companies in control of retail food.

Walmart may be evil. But, they are less evil than Pepsi and Coke and are the only planetary force able to stand up to them—and they have. One of the reasons why mom & pop markets, and eventually supermarket chains, will fall before operations like Walmart and upscale versions like Wegmans, is that only when operating at such a scale may a retailer negotiate terms with the multinational beverage giants, or, better yet, bottle their own poison.

I used to work for Pepsico as a merchandiser. Pepsico is the umbrella for Pepsi/Fritolay. When I bought a Coke and brought it on the truck my boss had a cow, and informed me that we would be fired if caught drinking it. On the side of every Fritolay chip box was the Pepsico symbol, two praying hands engulfing the globe. Pepsico and Coke are evil empires that utilize the kind of corporate iconography that one would expect to find on a James Bond spoof like Get Smart.

Years later, when I walked into my first meeting with the soft-drink overlord's emissary my boss,

The Ghetto Grocer

Andy the independent store owner, was shaking in fright, knowing that he was being bent over the economic barrel. In this annual economic sodomy ritual both soda empires sent in their local economic hit men to announce that our prices would be going up again. If we expanded their cooler space—at the expense of selling profitable food items—our prices would only go up as much as every other outfit. If we did not 'play ball' our prices would go up more, and we would be relegated to competing with convenience stores instead of grocery stores. These suited pricks admonished us when our single serve sales went down. When I suggested that we kick the bastards out and sell locally bottled items and micro-brew sodas at deep discounts, and try to carve out a hometown niche, Andy looked at me like he was Himmler and I was Goering, and I had just suggested kicking Hitler in the nuts.

The bottom line is the people you buy sodas from do not make the profit. The money slides right up the pyramid to the multinational beverage companies, all because you love that wrapper. The only beverages that your neighborhood retailer— or even Walmart for that matter—make any coin on are the off brands. In retail food the big brands that you have to have: Bounty; Kraft; Hellman's; any name-brand cereal; Tide; Pepsi; Coke are handled gratis by the retailer. Everything you grew up wanting based on advertising becomes a 'loss leader' to the food retailer by the time you are a full grown toddler.

The insane byproduct of 1950s brainwashing called 'brand loyalty' is the primary reason why grocery store employees that made $12 an hour in 1993, make $9 an hour in 2013. A generation of wage slaves is toiling below the poverty line because this planet of giant brain washed toddlers sucking on their toxic bab-bas have to suck from the bottle decorated in the package they were conditioned to equate with quality when they were children.

Cheap and Selfish Beats Stupid and Loyal

Aluminum and plastic are not stable materials. They leach and dissolve, particularly at and above room temperature. Buy some Mexican Coke in a glass bottle and taste test it against the American Coke in the PET nipple. Taste with your mouth instead of your eyes. Even though the overpriced imported Mexican stuff was bottled with rat piss and water from sources where the Mexican Army and drug gangs routinely dump bodies, it still tastes better than the poison you are in love with.

If you are actually concerned with how much you are spending on this stuff, this is what I do. I spend $20 per week on groceries. I drink tap water and coffee made with tap water. I can walk around the lake where my water comes from if I want to, and have. I occasionally buy glass bottled juices bottled by small outfits, which have screw tops. I clean and refill my glass bottles with tap water and keep them cold. When I have brewed too much coffee I pour it hot into a clean bottle and screw on the lid. The bottles seal, and the coffee stays fresh for at least six months, and makes better tasting iced coffee than anything I have had at a restaurant short of Thai Coffee.

The best part is I don't have to haul all of that water weight home from the store. If you did not drive, and had to carry everything you consumed, you would realize what a good idea piping water in is, as opposed to bottling and carrying it. It is no accident that civilizations have usually been built, since the Neolithic age, on hydration systems that utilize gravity-powered or pressurized channels, just like the planet we live on does. Putting that stuff in a container and hauling it was the first bad stone-age idea that stone-age people did away with.

We are now living on a planet where our rulers sanction, and we subsidize, the most profitable bad idea to be reinvented by a race of regressively stupid apes. This race of stupid apes is all the more foolish for thinking themselves superior to their distant ancestors, who got sick of having to marry extra females just to have enough hands on deck to haul water up from the river. The smartest dude in history was the guy that designed a pipe so he would only have one wife nagging him at dinner time rather than three synchronized menstruation vectors hissing in his ear while he desperately tried to get drunk!

You might wish to read The Most Coveted Stuff below on this blog.

Apocalypse Pantry Update: Lengthening The End Time Gravy Train

© 2013 James LaFond

Across America there are a surprising number of people in all walks of life currently planning for a social catastrophe of some kind. Weather it is a pandemic; a solar flare that takes out the power grid for a month or more; or the eruption of Mount OMG, the concern that our society is so near the end of a barely sustainable cycle, has many folks looking at their own resources or banding together with like-minded people to form contingency networks.

My print publisher Paladin Press has long sold titles devoted to surviving bad times. Even the History Channel recently did a dark docudrama about a family surviving social breakdown. My nonfiction writing has tended to focus on surviving the crappy nuances of the here-and-now. Much to my surprise I was contacted by a small local group of suburban professionals; husbands and wives with kids and establishment jobs, not some tobacco-chawing redneck with a wall-eyed wife, about help with their security arrangements.

What I found was a suburban house like any other, with the exception of high quantities of very sustainably repackaged groceries in the basement, and a handbook written by an x-military guy who specializes in advising people who have these concerns. I have not yet gotten a copy of the book and will do so and post a review. During our two-hour discussion I did read some passages in the book about things I was very knowledgeable about, primarily the retail food industry; the nodes of which will constitute the first line of supply during any natural or manmade disaster. This is a good way to assess an author's knowledge depth—by going right to your specialty.

The man was spot-on with his assessment of the supply capacity of retail food outlets being critically short. I forget what his exact claim was, but it was an average that I agreed with. Let me break it down to you in a couple different ways. I will use normal business days as a measuring stick. We also have two other depletion rate models: food stamp surges when the ubiquitous mothers of future drug lords sally forth in droves from their lead-painted abodes to buy a month's worth of food in one unsavory swipe of their 'independence card'; and snow panics, during which you would think that The End Time is upon us already—except for the fact that DVDs and snack food outsell milk and bread.

Food stamp surges in urban markets double daily business.

Snow panics triple or quadruple daily business.

Milk & Bread

All stores, no matter their scale or their format, seek to keep a two-day's supply of milk and bread on hand. They would prefer to only have to house a one-day supply, as 'feshness sells'. But Sunday deliveries cost more, and then there are the intermittent holidays to consider—always a disaster to your food retailer. So two days it is. This means extra big orders are required to cover food stamps and snow panics.

Now, if Mount OMG has just erupted you at least have a snow scare on your hands—one day people, before there is nothing left to smear your rug rats' peanut butter and jelly on and nothing for them to wash down that now extinct repast but the mud coming out of your kitchen tap.

Perishables

Okay, the refrigerated stuff is stored at minimal levels because of product longevity and storage space concerns. All of these supplies can be regarded as being at milk and bread levels. Of course, if the power grid goes down, it's all mush anyhow. So what is the point? If something really crappy happens with the power grid or society, your emergency purchases—or looting, depending on whether or not you are a righteous ghettoite—is best focused on grabbing produce items that require no refrigeration: potatoes; apples; bananas. These are also the produce items that are often bought in pallet quantities. If it is a root, or it can survive a fall from a tree, it will last.

The Groceries

Dry groceries in the store center are set for a minimal three-day supply, because the guys who stock it are specialized and hard to train and are also drunks, drug addicts and criminals who call out once a week, or get locked up for verbally equating cops to farm animals on their way to work on Friday night. So the best selling items, like the top name brand mayonnaise, or the whole grain life-saver shaped cereal with the pedophilic bee on the box, is pretty much gone half way through day three. This means, that in the case of a run on supermarkets, your kids' favorite items and the goo that your wife just can't stand being replaced on her sandwich, will be gone. Good luck homeboy, it is looking like a long apocalypse already!

Fortunately there are three factors that make store stock higher than perceived. Keep in mind, that I have opened unsupplied stores that have survived two days of disaster-level blitz panic shopping and still found tons of food on the shelves. In monetary terms a neighborhood supermarket in a 1970s building holds from 0.2 to 0.4 million dollars in stock. Major outlets like a chain supermarket on a county crossroads hold from 0.5 to 1.0 million dollars worth. I've never worked beyond that scale and have to guess at over a million dollar inventory for the new mega markets.

1. Most mid-selling items will be overstocked by the clerk, and they represent a full third of your inventory. Off brands of beans, cereal with amateur

level cartoons, Miracle Whip [see Whipped! on the Harm City page] and, in the ghetto, anything that is not sweetened or heavily salted, are 'runners': items that can be let run without ordering for a week. This facilitates product rotation and helps one judiciously plan his hangover order.

2. 'Dogs', 'weird shit' and 'oddball items' are terms used to describe gourmet or specialty foods; expensive, slow selling delicacies sought out by that gay teacher shopping on his way out of town. It might comfort you to know that the last meal that can be got from a run-over food retailer at The End Time will feature the best exotic garnishes and most potent Asian condiments! The most nutritious items in this category are peanut butter substitutes made with soy, filberts, cashews and almonds. **Urban Shopper Note:** 'Yo, if you be lootin' grab dat shit!'

3. Wholesaler Sodomization of the ankle-grabbing retailer is a constant theme in retail food. In fact, the most used metaphor in retail food is sodomy of the traditional penitentiary kind, followed by gang rape metaphors. Really, you will hear a buyer talking to a seller back in the stockroom, and swear that you are listening to two thugs negotiate a drug buy. The fact is your local retailer, if an

independent, is choking on stuff he could not really afford to buy just so he can keep his prices down and remain viable. If it is a chain outfit the onsite manager is just the submissive partner in this massive inequitable sex metaphor. There is huge pressure from the wholesaler to buy single palletized items in large quantity. This brings us to the reason for this article, the fact that the economy has gotten so lousy for retailers that they are altering their inventory control model.

'My Money Doesn't Make Money Anymore'

Up through the 1970's supermarkets were constructed with significant storage space, up to 30% of total footage. Beginning in the late 70's the expansion of product lines began requiring evermore display space, causing the stockroom to decrease in size and deliveries to increase in frequency. By the 1980's, at least in the Baltimore area, you had one or two specialists in each store that was charged with making sure this week's promotion sold down enough to make room for next week's promotion, without selling out.

This effort to 'turn inventory over' every week was not just spatial, but financial. Handling inventory was risky, and labor intensive, especially when 20% of your stock was packed in glass! I have seen mountains of tiered soda pallets tumble like dominos, the food clerk's version of a tsunami-causing coastal landslide. The fact is, the dude that owned that 1980's market could either pay his clerks, and his utility company, and eventually the municipality [in the form of inventory tax] for the privilege of owning this resalable product, or he could give his money to some prick in a suit who would use that money to make more money, without having to pay a grunt to push it around.

This dual impetus for 'turning over stock' evolved into 'inventory control' and gained crucial momentum in the early 1990's when WallMart headed east into Maryland. A regional food retailer imported an eccentric Midwestern retailer to take up the CEO mantel and prepare to battle the retail food Goliath. I was one of the inventory control specialists recruited for this effort. This outfit was so streamlined that we had no stockroom to speak of, and my specialty largely involved the ability to 'freight' [merchandise onto shelves] vast orders of perishable groceries before they thawed out, as it went from truck to floor overnight, without enough storage to accommodate the order.

But the product selection began reproducing at a rate that would have been envied by our food stamp customers, and even those stores with vestigial stockrooms and spacious sales floors are now inadequate; the more so when one considers the new pressure in retail food, the reversal of the 'bounteous suit' paradigm. As my boss's boss's boss's boss recently said when the complaint about stuffing our stockroom to the ceiling came to him, "It's money in the bank."

The translation is this: For an almost [not liquid] millionaire who holds significant local retail space, investing money with a suit or his online equivalent is perilous, and storing it in the bank is a guaranteed loss once inflation takes its bite. But, thanks to inflation, the can of beans we bought in September 2012 for 1.34 to redeem at a retail value of 1.79 is now valued at 1.99.

The result is a five-day supply on hand [up from three days] of a lot of food staples, most prominently the one thing you will need if the power grid and the water purification system in your area goes down for a week or more: bottled water. We retailers have gotten the news from On High from the manufacturers through the suppliers that water prices will continue to rise. They are buying heavily and inducing us to buy against a promised price hike.

Now there is something to wash down that last can of goose liver pate you find in the sheet metal wilderness that used to be your local grocer's specialty food aisle.

Ghetto Note

Homeboy, that Korean grocer with the pump shotgun down on the corner only has about a 12-hour supply of everything, and is probably already out of the barbecue flavored chips anyhow. Besides he's up-charging to pay for his body armor and counter shield. You might as well use your white-dudes-in-wigs to buy your liquor from him, and then, while he's dealing with some hard-headed fool, pile in his van with your homeboys and cruise on out to the county to do your looting. The white dude that runs that joint out there is only armed with a case-cutter. Remember Bro, when the grid goes down, yo baby's mamma's plastic ain't gonna swipe.

Bon appetite!

Ghettonomics: A Humanitarian Mission for Vsauce Michael, the YouTube Science Nerd

© 2013 James LaFond

I recently put up a link on our network page to Vsauce, an apparently commercially viable YouTube channel. Vsauce features the quirky and clearly enunciated 'face casts' of Michael, the most expressive nerd on the planet. I have recently viewed a half dozen of these five to fifteen minute science lessons on subjects as diverse as kissing, clothing, maximum human size, interstellar travel, the atmosphere, and the world-wide money supply.

On my way to work last night I was wracking my brain trying to figure out a readable little angle for a short article promoting Vsauce. As I took my seat on the bus in front of a young lady dressed in black tights and a leopard skin vest, speaking on her purple smart phone, I deployed my paystub envelope, which I save to take notes on, and began scribbling possible titles. I was not, however, to be granted the peace-of-mind required, as this young lady's every concern, her every trial and tribulation, was spoken into my ear.

That's right Baby Girl, you got between me and my subject, so now you are the subject, and it occurs to me, that Michael, the Vsauce science nerd, may be just the man to offer a solution to your woes, as varied as they are. His bits seem inspired by viewer questions. So, if you managed to pick up that Harm City card I left on the seat next to you, and found your way here, then find your way to the Vsauce link and ask Michael if he can wax empirical on any of the subjects brought to light by you discourse with the man-child sex drone that is ineffectually keeping your house, while I pay for your community college education, and your mother raises your baby's daddy's child*. I'm thinking the pizza question is a good start.

So Baby Girl, in case you forgot the substance of your sublime discourse, which you conducted on a staggeringly advance technological wonder that was never even predicted by the likes of L. Ron Hubbard, Isaac Asimov, Arthur C. Clarke, Larry Niven, or NASA when I was your age, I have recorded the salient portions for you, on my lowly envelope and the paystub within, and am transcribing them now...

The Ghetto Grocer

Fool

"Look, I been workin' my ass off in school all day, so you need ta take care of the food situation since I ain't about to come home hungry en remain hungry! You feel me?"

"I know the EBT card ain't loaded yet, but dare be change layin' around—If that R-Jay hasn't pocketed that shit. Besides, you got that small ass no good loaf of potato bread that you should not have bought no how, which needs to be returned. Return that shit for some real bread en make us a sandwich."

"Where am I? I don't know yet. Okay, I am at the library. Look, they havin' a pajama story time right here... No fool, we ain't goin'!"

"Because It's for children jackass!"

"No, I am not goin' to the store tonight. You know I have to be up tomorrow early to get my hair straightened. You know how I get when my hair is not straight!"

"What you mean they no mayonnaise left? Now you know we can't be lettin' R-Jay make no sandwiches and still have mayo at the end of the month. That fool is heavy with the spoon you know. So I guess you need to take that change en get some mayo too!"

"What do you mean you want me to go too? Fool we sharin' the same bus ticket en I ain't kickin' out another sixty cent so you don' have to ride alone!"

"Shoot, you the man of the house ain't you? So get out there en get us somethin' to eat!"

"Oh that's right, the store a whole half a mile away! Okay, how much money you got, without returnin' the potato bread?"

"Okay five dollars ain't goin' ta get us a pizza delivered from no Steevarinos. I don't know how that is even legal; advertizin' a five dolla cheese pizza en den not even deliverin' it? You know that ain't right! Okay, check that new pizza joint up the way, whatever-they-call-it, online."

"What! R-Jay let a Trojan Horse up in my computer! What was R-Jay doin' up on my computer anyhow?"

"Okay, okay; I don't even want to know!"

"No. I am too tired to ride around on this bus again and pick up that pizza. You know dey pizzas be good—you could go and get us a pizza right now!"

"No, that is out of the question."

"Why? Why! Because fool that five-dolla cheese pizza is clearly not big enough for three."

"Listen fool, eight slices do not split three ways, and if we let R-Jay go get the pizza then we got to spilt it with him, and that is not happening."

"Okay, I'm getting' off at my stop right now. I'm sleepy, noxious and angry!"

And every time I looked up there was an adoption poster that, in a sane world, you might have taken notice of.

Reader's Note: I don't know about you, but I'm an R-Jay fan.

*I did not have enough space on the envelope and stub to record the childcare discussion, which clearly indicated that the maternal grandmother was footing the bills and doing the work.

Whipped! Do Not Move in with Your Baby's Mamma until You Read This

Last night was an unseasonably cold spring night; a bad time to be suddenly homeless. I ran into three of these guys last night: one suffering from tremors and catatonic, sliding ever more silently into insanity; another heaving up his guts on the sidewalk and begging me to cash his check for him using my identification, for which consideration he was willing to part with $200. The third fellow was freshly roofless, employed, and about 30 years old, an HVC tech. I usually see him in the morning. His name is Tyrice.

Tyrice was shivering, riding a long low alcohol buzz, and sitting long-faced and surly as he waited for the cab he had called. He was going to sleep on his boss's porch. That would save him a two-bus commute to meet him in the morning, and, well...Tyrice was still angry, smoldering, and saw in me a kind shoulder to use as a sounding board. The decades of interviews, it seems, have forged my demeanor into that of the People's Psychologist.

Tyrice gives me a lilting shrug, "Say brother, it's a bitch out here—specially when yo Baby's Mamma put ya here!"

"I've been there my man—was fired by my wife in Oh-three."

Tyrice warms up to me and scoots a little closer, "Led me ask you then, juz sayin'. Juz say dat you a workin' man—which you iz—en you got the morning commute, en you in a hurry to meet up with the boss, en you in a hurry for breakfass too, so ya make a sausage en mustard sandwich. That's reasonable right? You don't make no mess, don't wake no body..."

The People's Psychologist is now nodding his head sagely as the victim of Estrogen Oppression forges on into a hand-gesture supported dialogue, "En juz sayin' you come home, after a hardddd day crawlin' up dem ducts, en the Baby's Mamma be waitin' hands on hips, chin out hea', mo sass den ass, 'What you doin' makin' but one sandwich in the morning when dey two mouths ta feed!'"

"En juz sayin' you tryin' ta make omenz—but naaaaah, shit got to get raw up in dere, 'Don't 'Baby' me! Bring me a B-L-T!'"

"En you like, 'Okay Baby a BLT, comin' right up.'"

The People's Psychologist gives a sympathetic nod and Tyrice picks his next words carefully, in order to elicit maximum empathy and male outrage, "En juz sayin' you know, you got the playbook, workin' da Baby Mamma Playbook, but you in a hurry and mistake the Miracle Whip fo mayonnaise, en she like, 'Oh hell no! This shit is nasty—some purposeful nasty shit!' like you tryin' to poison her en shit."

Tyrice makes sure to gloss over the sentence or two of ill-conceived and poorly chosen objections to his live-in food critic's critique of his gourmet refrigerator door dinner, and cuts directly to the results, "En here I iz, freezin' my behind off out in this cold joint, waitin' on a cab dat's late."

The People's Psychologist agrees, "Yeah, it's a cold night to be on the street."

The Ghetto Grocer

Tyrice, sure now that he has a sympathetic ear, spreads his hands and shrugs his shoulders, "Now I ask you Sir, was I wrong?"

The People's Psychologist, prepared as if for a daytime TV appearance before an 86.5% female audience, levels the accusatory finger at the younger victim of Estrogen Oppression, "Of course you were wrong!"

Tyrice flashes the old traitor a hurt look, "Say what!"

His counselor amplifies the ages' old point, "You are the dude, so you have to be wrong. If you were right, that would make her wrong, and she can't be wrong because she is the chick!"

Tyrice then drops his shoulders and looks down at the cold hard floor, "So that's the way it is huh?"

The third man on the scene walks by with a snort, "Shoot, he hasn't figured that out by now! Hell I learned that the first year! The woman is always right."

Having my verdict confirmed by another veteran of the gender wars helped me feel better about giving the young man a hard way to go. Later, into the early morning, I could not help but think of poor Tyrice every time I walked by the mayo section. There's always a bright side though. I bet those forced air ducts are feeling cozy today compared to yesterday, in that time before Miracle Whip, when Tyrice actually had a bed to sleep in.

Men, let us not forget Tyrice, the Miracle Whip Martyr; another fallen soldier, on the street again.

Thursday, April 4, 2013

Ghetto Grocer #1: Nastay Monay

© 2013 James LaFond

I have become known as a writer to the extant I have largely thanks to my Harm City work, primarily dedicated to urban violence and the survival lessons to be learned therein. Years ago my father, disturbed by my subject matter, suggested I write supermarket handbooks for employees and customers. I responded, "The employees can't or won't read, and the owners would never put something out for sale that would educate their customers, as they depend on their ignorance. It is a non-starter Dad."

Andy Boy

Four years ago, as the general manager of a ghetto supermarket, I did write a handbook for my perishable grocery crew. One of them actually read it, and then read it to the others. They all seemed pleased that their education in the finer points of their trade, lowly though it may be, rated such attention from 'The Man'; the aggregate mythic status of all white oppressors having been attached to my person by the inhabitants of the tiny indoor plantation I ran on behalf of some spoiled middle-aged rich kid. 'So much for my illiteracy theory', I thought, glad in this instance to be proved overly cynical.

The owner though was enraged, that he, with his master's degree, had not been consulted. When I noted that he had been working on his own handbook for the past 15 years, and that I desired a functional crew 'yesterday, not fifteen years from now' he became unglued and began snarling as his tiny fists beat on the table and he whined about 'giving them [employees] the wrong idea' [as to their worth, or lack there-of]. Even as he bemoaned their cataloging skills and rudimentary customer service gutturals, he still clung to his lone educated status as something separating himself from the 104 of 'them' that he found his self-doubting identity threatened by at that most primal level. Andy could not bear to think his staff was even capable of reading, let alone willing to take a part in educating themselves in the high art of retail food management...

The Ghetto Grocer

So here it is; my belated piecemeal guide to your ghetto shopping experience. Oh yes, Andy, and the rest of you literate suburban primates are surely mumbling under your repressed breath, "I do not shop in the ghetto, so what exactly is your point?"

My point friends, urbane snobs and bland suburbanites, is that wherever you shop, short of the overpriced gourmet shopping experience that less of you can afford with each shopping year, that you are in fact shopping in a ghetto export outlet. If it ends in 'Mart' it is a slice of the ghetto, designed to bring the ghetto to you and the ghettoites to it. If it is a 'supermarket' anywhere financially south of Half-million-dollar Prefabricated McMansionville, than you are shopping with an outfit that could not stay in business without the EBT cash, food stamps, WIC vouchers, and 'independence cards' that constitute the modern Welfare Mamma Carbocracy.

If you are just a blog reader, and have not made it to the Harm City page, think of the Ghetto Grocer as a public service to you; my humble attempt to keep you in the low know. If you have any questions concerning shopping for your food feel free to address them to me, your Hood-friendly Ghetto Grocer, via the comments function at the bottom of this and every other Ghetto Grocer installment. In the meantime, Welcome to Ghetto-Mart, and enjoy your purchase—"Wait, what you got in your pocket son!"

Ghetto Name Hall of Fame Entry

"'Arrcka': A, R, R, C, K, A—her mother should be shot! This came through on the Money Gram receipts this morning. Can you imagine that illiterate bitch—sitting there in the maternity ward waiting to drop this kid so her mother can raise her and she can go lay down with another man—thinking to herself, 'How many consonants can I use to misspell Erika?'"

-Miss Ezz, Cheap Guys R' Us

Nastay Monay

Being a bus patron I strive to keep neatly folded one dollar bills in my wallet to facilitate ease of boarding; not wanting to be the fool that spends five minutes trying to shove crinkled up bills into the fare meter. Toward this end I ask the cashiers that wait on me in various ghetto-marts for 'good ones'. This has recently resulted in various stories being related to me by these cashiers as to the foulest bills they have been called upon to handle. If ever you see a cashier handling money with gloves on, you might want to keep the following tales of ghetto exchange in mind.

Homeless Sock Money

"We had this one smelly old dude—thankfully I was just bagging—who peeled down this sweaty sock that was so dirty it was the color of his leg, and pulled out a flap of folded bills. They were soaking wet and had to be peeled apart slowly. Jen showed it [the twenty-dollar bill] to me when she closed. It even had crystallized body salts stuck in the crease. I don't know what he was going to do with the bills she gave him as change: I guess start a new sock wad of cash."

-Decker

Butt Money

"I was at the fireman's bull roast with Woody. We had a naked stripper on each table and hookers in the bathroom stalls blowing you for twenty bucks—blowing hundreds of guys. You could not even piss there were so many cops and firemen lined up for blow jobs. Well Nadia was dancing on our table and Woody fell in love. She picked up all the bills with her ass and her snatch; just throw them on the table and 'whap, snatch', it's up her cooch. So Woody is all drunk, lays his head back on the table, spreads a five dollar bill across his mouth, and thrusts his tongue through the bill—fucking murdered Lincoln all over again—and Nadia squats down on his face and the bill is gone. I was done eating, I can tell you that."

-John

Breast Money

I did have one run in with a stripper at a black night club that Duz took me to. She was about six foot and 250. Duz thought she was the greatest and described her in the following glowing terms, 'The girl with the giant jelly ass and tits like trashcan lids'. She was pretty, and had a nice soft voice. But when a girl that big is dancing for an hour in a crowded bar, and she presses up against you to get her tip and put it in her felt Crown Royal bag she has a tendency to stick to you. The girls in this club were also rough. The giant Amazon chick actually threw Duz to the concrete floor and molested him while the drug dealers tipped him!

So, while my bodyguard was being ravaged by this gigantic Tina Turner knock off the big sweaty girl slid up to me looking for a kiss. I was actually afraid that my face would get stuck between her breasts and I would die of asphyxiation. I just pressed the bill against her upper breast, and she smiled, and wiggled away, dancing, the bill never leaving its place. I swear George was smiling at me as he bounced away...

Recently I discussed this subject with a ghetto cashier: "The breast money is not only nasty, it is more common this time of year [summer] than purse money. I had this welfare mamma earlier who had her smart phone, her pack of cigarettes, her independence card, and her cash all in one breast cup of her bra. I wouldn't have been surprised if she pulled ten items or less out of the other one. It is so disgusting because it is always wet, and you have to handle it twice, once to count it, and once to sort it, and then again to count out at the end of the night. Thank God for hand sanitizer!"

-Mary

Crotch Money

"Okay, you get a lot of balled up sweat pants money, but it isn't wet.

"The breast money is disgusting and is probably the most common form of storage. When you are wearing tights and your ass is as wide as the register lane, where the hell are you going to put a wallet? Most breast money is sweaty or even soaked—thank God I don't work afternoons! The breast money you get in the morning is usually powdered. They do powder up. The sistas do have their pride when it comes to their gigantic boobs.

"What kills me though, is crotch money. Every once in a while—I'd say one in ten—you get a sista who has either got too much other shit jammed in her breast, or is flat, and has to fold her money up in her underwear. I suppose if you are wearing tights or sweats and you aren't equipped with the standard giant boobs, then you have no choice but to put you nasty money in the sweaty poof pouch of your nasty panties! And there I am unfolding this crotch money, which is not only wet like breast money but crinkled up like sweat pants money! Get a life—or better yet a job—you muffin top cows!"

The Ghetto Grocer

-Miss Ezz

Thanks for shopping with your ghetto grocer, and please ladies, remember to purchase your smart phone covers over at the courtesy booth for only nine-ninety-nine.

Ghetto Grocer #2: Bachelor Party at Parcel Pickup

© 2013 James LaFond

I was talking to my fellow night crew grunts last night and found out that this past Saturday two young ladies entertained them from just after 4 to just before 5 AM, on the front sidewalk. I also heard that 'The Man' was not pleased with the backup night captain letting this go on in front of his establishment for an hour. I got this from three different sources, so permit me to regale you.

Mysteria, the gay cashier, was working up front when Lily, the elderly deli clerk, came in early from her break and mumbled something about two young women saying something impolite on the sidewalk. One woman was wearing a blouse and short black shorts, and the other was wearing a denim dress. The lady with the dress was pulling down her top and lifting her dress to get Mysteria's attention.

The Ghetto Grocer

Both of the ladies were described as 'twentyish' and 'attractive'. The one in the dress lifted it once to admit the head of her crouching friend. The call then went out across the aisles that 'lunch' was indeed being served at 'parcel pickup'.

By the time the night crew made it up front the lady in the dress was sporting a 'flesh-colored' strap-on electronic vibrator and her friend was pretending it was a flute. These things and other antics continued for about a half hour until Mysteria finally got a phone number from one of the performers.

The Sun Paper vender then pulled up and began filming the action, even requesting a variety of positions from the young starlets. Soon though, Joe, the grocery manager, pulled up on the lot. Mysteria advised her new flung friends to leave. There was a hitch in their plan as they walked off past Joe. The vibrator did not apparently have a limp setting and was making something of a vertical tent out of the dress.

Joe looked at the ladies and indicated that they were leaving in a suspicious state. I forget what wording he used with them as he told me while we were rotating The Man's Greek yogurt. He did tell me that the offending prostheses disappeared beneath the dress head first, and as the hydraulic duo walked off the lot the cord and the control stick were dangling beneath the hem of the denim dress.

Concerned for my boss' peace-of-mind I offered to recommend a bouncer and a barker to help these ladies formalize their act and bring in more overnight costumers. This did not find favor with management, and the night captain was directed to, "Tell them to leave, and if they don't, call nine-one-one and tell them that two girls are having sex on the sidewalk. The cops might take fifteen minutes if it is an armed robbery. But if the word goes out that you have two hot chicks in need of night sticks, you will have the entire precinct here in fifteen seconds!"

Ghetto Grocer #3: Fort Hood-Rat

© 2013 James LaFond

The 'ghetto grocer' you say.

Who really goes to a ghetto grocery store you may wonder.

So you doubt the existence of The Realm of Squalor do you?

Perhaps you assume that your tax money is shipped directly from O'Sauron's overflowing vaults, in the form of food and goods, to the heroic oppressed shivering or sweating—depending on the season—in their dismal urban dens. I ask you, did the actual Dark Lord, the omnipotent genius which the current occupant of the Tower of Power merely imitates, send care packages to his orks and goblins, trolls and Easterlings? No, he did not! He set them loose upon the land and bade them scavenge at the expense of his enemies.

The following tales of insane behavior come from Joel's Stop, Shop & Rob, a low-end discount joint in the hood: otherwise known as Fort Hood, Baltimore, located in the Mid-Eastern Territories...

Jesse

Jesse, the grocery manager, was on duty one evening, when a pack of hood-rats broke into the courtesy booth and began robbing the till. He called the cops and then locked them in the booth. As they shoved on the door from the other side he pressed his back against it. The spryest hood-rat among them leapt over the wall and shot Jesse in the leg, permitting his compatriots to escape over Jesses' prostrate form.

Joel

Mister Joel was robbed at gunpoint in the store. Being a good citizen of the Fraternal Order of Retail Food Honcho's, he took the very clear security film to colleagues, so that their loss prevention people might examine it and be on the lookout for the gunman. He soon found out that the film of him being startled and robbed at gunpoint had become a diversionary tonic of sorts among his peers, who sat around laughing at Joel's plight, and replaying it for friends. I remain woefully uninformed as to the brands of snack foods consumed at these viewings.

On one occasion, Joel, an older man, tackled a shoplifter running off with his goods. He wasn't the accountant he once was and was having difficulty holding onto the hood-rat's hind-quarters as they rolled on the sidewalk. He called for help. His help came in the form of Patsy, 'not the brightest bulb in the pack'. Patsy darted inside, grabbed a gallon of milk, came back out on the sidewalk, and emptied it on the shoplifter's head—another $2.99 down the drain...

Missy

Missy was running a register while a young mother and heroin addict [in this hood 8 out of 10 white residents are heroin addicts] was drinking from her 'baby's sippie cup'. The baby seemed very happy, and it was discovered that the cup they were sharing was filled with vodka. The addict was on her federal flip phone cursing a stream of profanity to the 'baby's daddy'. This impelled Delvin, the security guard, to eject her.

Dunbar Rocks!

Thelma was running Register #5 recently [late July 2013] when an unusual number of normally broke ghettoites flooded the store. These people normally have very little of anything to spend late in the month, as the food stamps are generally gone by the 20th. The people were smiling and thanking, 'God', 'dem Dunbar bankers', and 'dat fool driver who foget to lock da back doe!'

As it turns out the backdoor of a Dunbar truck came open at 30 MPH just down the street from Fort Hood. A box of money bounced out and burst on the centerline of the busy secondary street, and the ghetto erupted as if for VJ Day 1945. The driver stood and watched as all of the money was looted, and the guard in the box stayed there with his shotgun primed to repel boarders. But, thank God, there had been more than enough money in that crate to purchase enough steamed shrimp at Fort Hood to feed the entire hood!

Molly

Molly is often accosted by panhandlers when coming and going to work, and while smoking on her break. She has recently learned that some live under the wood deck of the snowball stand across the street and scavenge the change that falls through the slats. Her stories of panhandler inconvenience and rudeness are legion. Lately, one of the most persistent beggars has invested in a guitar, "His tall goofy white ass stands on da cona strumin' his guitar while da two drug dealas dat owns him stand behind as if dey got a leash on 'is neck. En dare he is, as I walk by en da drug dealas sayin' 'Hey babay'. Dare he is, singin', 'I need a dollar 'cause I don't know where I am!'. His ass can starve singin'!"

There you go: a sample of the doings and deeds of the ghettoites and the overworked traders that man the Fort Hood Trading Post, exchanging corporate foodstuffs for the variously ill-gotten cash of the Barbarians of The Interior.

Ghetto Grocer #4: Food Handling Horror Stories

© 2013 James LaFond

"All men are pigs. I never let them handle exposed food."

-Miss Betty S., 1981

"I love this crap."

-late night food market customer, 2013

If only the customer above knew how close he was to the descriptive truth. There is a general medical myth common in the U.S. that there are a plethora of 'stomach viruses' out there that you catch like a cold and that give you loose bowels. What is usually happening when you find yourself running for the toilet is that something got into your food that should have been flushed down the toilet to begin with.

The Ghetto Grocer

The Right Hand of Illness

This article is not about overall store cleanliness, which deserves a piece all its own. What we are discussing is the personal cleanliness of the people handling your food, and how your food might be contaminated, especially if the highly-educated and well-compensated employee does not then put on clean cloves. But even if they do put on these gloves, if they tug a glove on with a feces-covered finger, and then use that gloved hand to mix your potato salad—throne of misery here you come. This has a lot to do with washing hands, and how food prep areas and bathrooms used by employees are maintained. Hence you see all of those hand washing signs in restaurant restrooms, reminding the employees to wash their hands.

As a grocery store manager I have been charged with enforcing cleanliness, hairnet use, and training janitors. Most store managers are not good at this end of the job because they have never been janitors, and did not come up working in food prep for long periods, but got funneled into their position through the two largest departments: the front end and center store [dry grocery.] What I found out immediately upon becoming a manger was that, all of a sudden, when I used the bathroom, everyone was washing their hands! It was my time as a lowly clerk that had taught me the reality. And being a writer, I'm the kind that takes notes just for curiosity's sake. According to my notes taken over the past 20 years, I can inform you of the following:

1. 9 in 10 janitors and bakers wash their hands after using the bathroom or the trash compactor

2. 7 in 10 dry grocery clerks wash their hands after using the bathroom or trash compactor

3. 5 in 10 meat cutters, seafood clerks and produce clerks wash their hands after using the bathroom or trash compactor

4. 3 in 10 deli clerks wash their hands after using the bathroom or the trash compactor

5. Only 5 in 10 of those employees who wash their hands do it properly

I have only been able to survey male employees, as I have always been a male. However, my janitors and female coworkers have forever complained that female restrooms are the filthiest, just by virtue of the fact that blood is added to the other bodily excretions smeared on the walls.

Bucky

Bucky was a mentally handicapped janitor who practiced great diligence cleaning Store #33. Not only did Bucky scrub the restrooms, mop and buff the floors, and sweep and hose the storefront, he made the morning coffee as well. What a swell guy Bucky was, always with a smile for his coworkers, particularly Mister Tony, who loved his morning coffee, always the first to get a cup. One morning, at 6:15 AM, on a Saturday, Bucky was behind making the coffee, cleaning up after the understaffed night crew as he was.

Mister Tony went looking for Bucky, who was probably cleaning the men's room, just as Eddie, the receiver, was using the urinal. 'Where was the commercial coffee pot', Mister Tony wanted to know? He would make the coffee himself since Bucky was behind. It just so happened, that Bucky was multitasking in the men's room when Mister Tony found him. As Eddie stepped away from the urinal and turned to the sink, Bucky beat him to it, with the scrub brush he had just used to scrub out the toilets in one hand, and the coffee pot in the other. Bucky ran the brush under running water for a moment, and then stood and scrubbed the pot out with it. As Tony opened the door he saw the method by which Bucky had always prepped the morning coffee pot, and 'Went ape-shit!'

Eddie had to restrain Mister Tony from strangling Bucky, as Bucky shed tears and cried that he always rinsed the toilet brush off before using it to scrub out the coffee pot! Eddie eventually corrected Bucky's notion of the purifying effects of running water. Mister Tony could not get over it though, and took over the coffee pot duties, as soon as he purchased a new pot.

Brown-back

This small, hairy, hunch-backed night clerk stunk so badly that I could not get anyone to work with him. We thought it was because of his rotten teeth, until he bent over and his shirt slid up his back and we saw the matted fecal matter on his back hair and the brown stained skin beneath. 'Big' Earl 'Bro Train' Johnson said, "What, does this dude shit his self and sleep in it?"

This finding added new horror to the dimension of this clerk's scratching of his back with his darkened finger nails. I reassigned him to work paper and detergent products, as in any given food aisle, there are food products that are consumed directly from the container or packaging without first being cooked at temperatures necessary to kill e-coli bacteria.

Pops

Pops was an old functional alcoholic, who was drunk for the entire two years I worked with him. I thought he was a 70 year old man with a tan. I was disabused of this notion by Big Nate, one day when it was raining, and Pops was afraid to walk out from underneath the storefront canopy. I thought his reluctance to walk was from old age, but Nate assured me that 'Pops' was only fifty years old. He then said, "Look" and pointed as Pops staggered out into the rain, and his face began to streak. Nate declared scornfully, "That dirty mutherfucker only takes a bath in June, when he gets his hair cut! And you know he never washes his hands. I can't believe they have him working the baby food."

Jorra

Jorra was an old dairy clerk with chronic sinus infections who wore the same dirty gloves every day of the week, every week of the year, until we would find them laying on the sink in the bathroom. The only time he removed his gloves was when he sat in the stall. He also used the backs of these gloves to wipe his nose as he worked. We made it our duty to occasionally follow him into the bathroom and throw the filthy things in the trash compactor.

Scabby Abby

Scabby Abby was a bakery clerk who cut cake, sliced bread, bagged bread and rolls, and boxed doughnuts, éclairs, and cookies. She had long hair and took off her hairnet anytime the manager was not around, which was most of the time as she worked the overnight shift. Abby refused to wear gloves, as she claimed they irritated her chaffed, cracked and sore-covered hands. You see Abby was a heroin addict who had open sores, which she picked at as junkies are want to do. When she would slice the bread I would look over my shoulder in disgust wondering how many of the flakes clinging to the slices were crumbs and how many skin flakes and scabs.

Abby also had false teeth. She would take out her false teeth and scrub them with her toothbrush on the food prep table behind the bakery counter, and use the sanitary sink to brush her teeth, rinse out her mouth, and apply her Fixodent.

According to female staff, Abby, who never wore sanitary gloves, also never washed her hands in the women's room, and sometimes had 'accidents' which necessitated her throwing her fouled underwear in the open trashcan, adding to the floral ambiance of the facility.

Abby was also a diabetic, who tested herself on the table used for bagging rolls and boxing doughnuts. Her coworkers repeatedly told me about her smearing blood on the table when she pricked herself with her testing pin. When working at this same table bagging and boxing confections she was prone to licking her fingers in order to clean the icing off of them in between boxes.

Scabby Abby was eventually fired after more than a year of service, not for mishandling food, but for eating stolen food.

Bon appetite!

Two Masked Gunmen: A Ghetto Grocer War Story

© 2013 James LaFond

Bill, the receiver at the Ghetto Depot, was opening up the back door in the morning while it was still dark. Two men in masks with guns rushed in and he ran like hell, out of the stockroom, through the store, and through the glass panel of the front door, and called 911.

The masked men then beat down the meat cutter. They also dragged the female bakery clerk into and down the frozen food aisle and beat her 'badly' enough that she required hospitalization. Her jewelry was taken, but there was no attempt to rob the store.

Both employees were hospitalized, and the police made no arrests.

The employee that gave me the tip thinks that this attack was in retaliation for the recent firing of seven hood-rat employees, three of whom were running a loan-sharking ring that preyed on, among others, a handicapped parcel pickup clerk, charging 300% interest on money loaned for cigarettes.

As a general note: I know of three recent newspaper stories involving men assaulting women in Baltimore City, allegedly at the request of other women—two of these incidents being shootings. Perhaps the Ghetto Depot raid above was an expression of this new form of feminine conflict resolution.

Ghetto Grocer #5: Foodstampable, Will The State Subsidize Your Party

© 2013 James LaFond

How do food stamps work?

These are no longer the paper food coupons of old. But in retail food—and in the benighted ghetto!—we yet name them so. We are talking about an 'EBT' or 'independence' card that will have a 'cash side' and a 'food side'. The cash may be taken out at the supermarket or other State money laundering operation and used to buy cocaine, heroin, crack, booze, lottery tickets, cigarettes, unregistered handguns, and all the other necessities of modern urban living.

When we talk about 'food stamps' these days we are discussing the 'food side'. In Maryland this money is distributed through The Department of Social Services. Depending on your need, your greed, and how well-placed your relatives are within The Department of Social Services, you: our humble hypothetical ghettoite, will receive between

$16 and $1,600 in 'food side' largesse. Now how may you spend this money?

If you are a dopefiend you simply lend the card and your pin number to a citizen in return for roughly half the cash. So, while your cash side money gets you face value dope, the food side money only gets you half the face value worth of dope.

Let's say you actually wish to dine rather than join the greater deluded society in its fitful slumber. What might you, Joe Ghetto, buy?

It is easier to note what you may not buy: anything that you cannot eat [or is not intended to be eaten by you] such as detergents, paper products, pet food, etc.; and any prepared foods that are purchased hot [They must be hot. If the retailer cooks it and then refrigerates it, you can buy it with your stamps. The State just does not want their money going to foodservice labor. They want you to at least have to heat the stuff up.]

Any other edible item is kosher on the State level. Even items such as candy and sodas, which have bottle and sin taxes leveled on them, are foodstampable. And, the best part is, you don't have to pay these taxes. Only that dumbass waiting in line behind you, who is actually working, has to pay bottle and snack taxes.

You are good to go. Now, before you head out to the local ghetto grocer's to begin wisely spending your lump sum of monthly food dollars, let me introduce your cashier: Queen Fo' Real. Queen is her real made-up-by-mamma ghetto name. The Fo' Real sobriquet she added herself, as an indication that she can be expected to 'tell it like it be!'

Queen Fo' Real is a cashier at Fort Hoodrat, who I met at the bar complaining of having 'T-Rex arms' from 'ringing up all them damn sodas en juices.'

Now that you too, Joe Ghetto, are one of the legions of ever-widening foodstampers let her tell it like it be:

"Stamps come out between the sixth en the sixteenth. I see so many fat people I don't even know what fat is anymore. Muffin top shit! Try a wedding cake top! Just yesterday there was this ghetto bitch in there giving her mother grief for using her food stamp card. You know the mother was buying food for the children while this bitch wanted to get high. The police won't come in on that shit. Security leaves same family female stuff alone. So after an hour of, 'Bitch this, bitch that', grandma came up in there and settled things."

"Security runs six-five three-fifty, at least; big muvs, one bigger than the other. Those little white junkies don't play that NFL shit with these boys. They are up for it, can't wait to tackle someone on the tile. There is very little theft. The only ones that ever fight are the females—straight up ghetto brawling bitches. The stupidest one was the skinny white boy junky who tried to steal a gallon of Tide. He was shittin' when Big Boy grabbed his ass and his feet couldn't even touch the ground to run. So many of the males are on parole, and have their parole I.D. on them, that they are all terrified of security."

"We had this one loser working in seafood who beat the shit out of his old lady. When the cops came for him he ran, and Big Boy took him down—hard! Shit, the cops didn't even get in the way—boom! These boys get bonuses for apprehensions. You do not want them to see you running."

"The largest order I rung up this week was six-hundred and thirty four dollars. She also had the largest remaining balance: eight-hundred and something. The typical order is three-hundred plus. We're talking about heaps of heavy shit. Who the fuck buys twenty-five pounds of sugar! I pick up so much of that shit I like to die. Who buys twenty-five pounds of sugar—a whole lot of people that's who!"

And don't think those bitches can't count. They might not be able to work, but they sure as hell can count. Shit don't look right, shit don't smell right, shit don't add up, they're commin' back! They might not pay for their food but don't try to take a fried chicken leg out of their hand! A penny, nickel, a dime, a quarter—and they are up in your ass! Back in the day, when they had to pay the bottle tax, this one bitch left her whole order of meat and everything sit in the lane and walked out, over having to pay seven cents in bottle tax. That's how people are when they don't have to work. They don't care about anything, not even feeding their babies."

As Queen regaled me with food stamp war stories I looked to my left out the bar door and saw two very rotund women, each carrying a stack of pizza boxes away from the pizzeria. They seemed serious, like people on a mission.

Queen finished off the interview by giving me a top-ten list of most rung items at her register for this, the foodstamp week of 9/9/13 to 9/14/13:

The Ghetto Grocer

1. Chicken, mostly by the 40 pound box

2. Pork, mostly chops in family packs

3. Fresh turkey wings

4. Canned collard greens

5. Smoked turkey parts [used to season the greens]

6. Frozen whiting fillets in a 5 pound bag

7. Dollar-priced beverages in 16 ounce bottles [usually in 1 to 4 case lots]

8. Dollar-priced snacks [chips, popcorn, cheese curls]

9. Ramen noodles

10. Dollar-priced frozen pizzas, entrees and sandwiches

As a cashier in Baltimore County in 2010 my most memorable food stamp order was purchased by an immensely fat white girl of about 18 years, who had a morbidly obese teddy bear drone with her. They purchased 37 dollars and some change worth of 50-cent snacks bags, heavy on the fake onion rings, along with a few bottles of Mountain Dew. In most cases, when the female food stamper runs out of money or has to pay for taxable purchases, the male drone produces a knot roll of twenty dollar bills and pays the balance.

This is just one of many ways in which State food subsidies seem inextricably linked to the cash drug culture. From the anecdotal evidence I have sifted it seems that black ghetto food stampers generally make healthier purchases than white suburban food stampers. Of course, there can be no urban-to-urban racial food purchase comparison, since poor urban whites don't appear to eat, but just bang drugs and drink booze.

The Bro Train: On The Extinction of Men

© 2013 James LaFond

Writers tend to portray themselves in a positive light, if only via the nature of our enterprise. I think it is about time to admit to a sin against my fellow man, and thereby accept some of the blame for this world we live in, where 'men' seem to be in such short supply. We live in a time when most of the adult males I know live off of women: mom, wife, daughter, girlfriend, grandma. By turn many of these women are living off The State, making these nominal males parasites upon parasites; not even reputable as second tier biological organisms go, let alone as social beings of the mind.

Let me set the stage:

The Bro Train

It was the early 1980s, and I was working on a supermarket night crew. One of my coworkers was actually a friend, a hardworking man who had been an elite high school athlete, and was black. At this time it was unusual for whites and blacks to be friendly in Baltimore. Race-based street fights over busing were less than a decade behind us. This man's name was 'Big' Earl 'Bro Train' Johnson. He had two fulltime jobs and rented two houses which he had renovated.

Earl took me on an urban renewal tour one time and pointed at a nice row of houses, "You see, that's what the white mayor is building for my people."

He then pointed to the other side of the street where the houses had been gutted for copper and aluminum, "And that is what these houses are going to look like after my people live in them for five years."

Earl was an interesting guy. He became even more interesting when we found out he liked men, particularly college-age men. Earl and I were both college-age ourselves, but had been working since sixteen, so were socially much older than our scholastic peers at work.

We got a new worker on the crew, a handsome young Italian guy. This caused Earl's decorum to crack. I had worked with him for two years and never knew he was gay until I heard him whisper across the aisles through the night, "Stallion, Stallion! Come to me my handsome Stallion!"

I was kind of surprised and let Earl know that I had had no idea. He responded, "No offense Jimmy, but I just can't get into your sawed-off Abe Lincoln lookin' self. You are not my type. I like that!" he said as he pointed to a frightened Mel, the young Italian rookie on the crew.

The Korean War vet who ran the dairy overheard this and said, "Hey Earl, my helper is a faggot."

He then looked at me and said, "Our [day crew] white faggot should get together with your [night crew] black faggot."

He then called for his assistant, "Hey Sweet Pants get over here."

The old timer than introduced the flamer and the masculine gay who had just stepped boldly from the closet. Earl's response was to pull a picture of himself in the nude from his wallet and show it to Sweet Pants [who was understood to be a catcher and not a pitcher]. Sweet Pants squeaked and literally ran and hid in the dairy cooler, as Earl laughed menacingly, "Shit, that little faggot, I'd send him back in here in a wheelchair with a bag strapped to his waist!"

We all thought it was crudely though frighteningly funny, and laughed. I had just recently established myself as someone who was respected and feared by the criminal elements on the street, and had cultivated a callous disregard for any weak men who could not take care of themselves. I never even considered questioning the ethics of Earl's intimidation of my other coworkers.

Some days later, in the middle of the shift, Mel came to me worried. Mel and I walked home together on occasion. He was only 18 and seemed to look up to me. He said, with a rabbit like fear in his eyes, "Earl just offered me three hundred dollars if I let him blow me in the bathroom. What should I do?"

I said, with all of my 22 or so years of wisdom, "If you have to ask me than I don't know you."

With that I callously walked away.

A few weeks later Mel quit work for no specified reason.

A month later he came in to visit the morning shift people as I was leaving, with a pretty blonde girl on his arm, announcing their engagement.

With that Mel fell off my radar screen as a weakling that had moved on to better himself through marriage, leaning on a woman to make his way in the world.

Twenty-five Years of Karma Later

I was working part time for a grocery store. On my afternoon off I was called in. I told them I would be there in two hours, which was the length of my bus commute. After my shift the assistant manager thanked me for coming in and offered to give me a lift home.

As he drove me home I found out he grew up in the neighborhood where I was now renting, the neighborhood I had just moved back into. I also discovered that his name was Mel. When I announced that I now knew where I remembered him from, he would not even admit to having worked with me at the neighborhood grocery store. I did not pursue the subject as he seemed upset, even shaken.

The Ghetto Grocer

After that night Mel never greeted me at work, and avoided contact with me. I also noticed him inappropriately touching a female staff member. Then he began making my work difficult, even at the risk of defying instructions from our draconian boss. This man would go to any lengths to sabotage my work station, even risking his standing with our employer.

This caused me to think back, to do some soul-searching, and to consider the concept of karma. I was now a post-management adult many times wiser in the ways of the world and the workplace than I had been as a young grunt. I had been called upon to hear sexual harassment cases. Indeed I had removed managers beneath me quietly when I found them acting unethically towards the men and women under them.

I can see through my own smudged rearview mirror that Earl [who was named 'Big Earl' for reasons other than height and weight] had been sexually harassing Mel. Mel had come to me, and I had turned away. Now, all those years later I was under him in a similar operation, and he was making my life as hard as possible; just behaving like a bitter scorned woman.

The Ghetto Grocer

As a savage young grunt, carving out my own violent image of manhood from a criminal working class environment, I had utterly failed on a social level to help Mel in his more feeble attempt to become a man. In those days Mel would have been laughed at by the employer and law enforcement. He looked to me as a more respected member of our crew, who was an influential friend to his abuser, to make it stop, and I laughed and turned away. In retrospect, I think the Bro Train would have laid off if I would have simply voiced some concern on behalf of Mel. Earl was not violent at all and was easy to reason with. I just chose not to.

Survive and Let Suffer

My austere, defiance-based, and violence-supported, ideal of manhood had liberated me, and me alone, it being a thoroughly selfish artifice for dealing with the alienation and exploitation of my marginal life. I am still largely that person: the man who steps over begging bums; who regards males as a gender as an enemy force pool; and who walks idly by while boys are stomped and beaten by other boys, justifying it all with a nod to Darwinian law.

The Ghetto Grocer

I think, every time that Mel makes life hard on me, that he is serving up some karma, in a primitive attempt to make me pay for being one of the people in his miserable life who through action and inaction, made of him someone socially far closer to a woman than a man. Every time I'm tempted to say, "Hey Stallion, what is your problem?" I remember that his problem, is at this stage, possibly insurmountable, and that I would not help him crawl out of his neutered abyss even if he asked.

I still, looking inside, find no compassion for Mel or his unfulfilling lot in life. His pathetic passive-aggressive workplace sabotage makes my cruel view that much more palatable as a value. Indeed, me being an hourly employee, I am materially enriched every time he deigns to meddle in my work and necessitates my working overtime.

I thought an hour ago, that my biggest sin concerning Mel had been my harsh refusal to aid him in our youth. After expressing our fleeting interactions over the decades and years, I think maybe my denying him the conversation that his feminized angst now seems to require of him, is probably the darker stain on my character.

The Ghetto Grocer

Upon reflecting as philosophically on Mel, Bro Train and me, as I am equipped to, I feel refreshingly barren of any care for he who I long ago helped push into the pit of his self-doubting feminized hell. I feel like a ruthless apostate who avoided the fate of some weaker aspirant to manhood; like a barbarian who has avoided the domestication that has befallen the whimpering hordes of his fellows who have been rendered merely male by the Mighty Mother of Lies called Civilization.

I am at peace with my stain.

Crumbs: A Ghetto Grocer War Story

© 2013 James LaFond

About five or six years ago, on a Sunday afternoon, I was working the front of the supermarket. Donny, the off duty cop that was handling security, was on the camera system, monitoring the store interior from the security office. I worked the front end displays, keeping an eye on the register for any customer service needs and greeting the customers. From this position I could see the store front, and preempt any panhandlers that came from the south.

I noticed that one of the hacks [illegal cabbies] was parked in the loading zone and went outside to tell him to move. When I arrived out front I noticed that the hack was speaking with a former coworker who had a great hatred for me, even though I had not fired him like so many of his fellows. He had faked an injury, quit his job, and then sued. I knew the man's wife was inside shopping so did not mind him loitering out front. But when I hit the lobby I could hear the f-words thundering. Then, when I hit the sidewalk to talk to the hack I said, "He guys, do you think you could clean up the language. Church just let out. We have families shopping here."

Even though only Jack, the former employee, was swearing, I asked both of them, just so Jack would not feel picked on, as he had a strong persecution complex.

Jack began screaming about being discriminated against because of his 'blackness.' I quietly stated that I was speaking to both of them and that I just wanted to maintain a family atmosphere. The hack moved off right away, not wanting to jeopardize my already marginal tolerance for his activity. Jack, however, continued to rant and rave, so I went inside, hoping that his wife would be checking out directly and get him off the lot by default. I did not want to have a scene, or sick Donny on him, because Donny was a cop and Jack was a con and they had some bad blood.

Sure enough Jack's wife was checking out when I came inside. Donny had seen the discussion on the security camera and came down by the coin machine to ask me if everything was alright. I told him that everything should be cool now that Jack's wife was leaving. As it turned out, that assessment was a bit optimistic.

The Ghetto Grocer

Jack came in stammering in a docile manner and his wife was on fire, giving me the 'what to' and the 'why for' over me 'racially profiling' her husband and not letting him wait on the front walk. I tried to explain that this was not the case, but she became increasingly angry. From that point I just kept voicing platitudes like, 'Did you find everything you needed Miss?' 'Is there anything else I can do for you?' and 'You have a nice day now.'

Donny was having a hard time suppressing his grin, when she raised her voice, "You, You! Who you callin' you, you!"

'You' Had been upgraded to a racist slur. This was hand-off time. On those occasions [about a third of the time] that a white person had a racial problem with Donny, I would step in. When a black person would have a racial problem with me [about a third of the time] he would step in. This is the only way to handle racial hatred. Once somebody becomes convinced that your behavior is racially motivated, they cannot be reasoned with. It is tougher to reason with a racist than a drunk or a crack head, as they have descended into pure emotion, with no capacity to reason.

The Ghetto Grocer

Donny stepped forward and ran interference as I stood calmly by. He spoke to her as she pointed and yelled at me, and Jack milled impotently about her heels. Finally, fed up with not being able to get me angry, Jack's wife pointed at Donny, and burst out, "You ought to be ashamed of yourself stickin' up for this cracka!"

She then pointed menacingly down at me [this was a big Amazon woman in high heels], "Hell, he ain't even much of a cracka—he's a crumb!"

She then turned on her heels and stormed out as we wished her a good day. We managed to hold it in until she got to the parking lot and then burst into laughter. We were thrilled with our new superhero crime-fighting identities: The Traitor and The Crumb. That kind of had a ring to it.

A racial harassment law suit was threatened. Donny vouched for my social handicap [being colorblind] and the threats were dropped.

'Don' Dey Know People Gots Ta Eat!': A Ghetto Grocer War Story

© 2013 James LaFond

On Saturday October 12 2013, at about 11:00 AM, the EBT [food stamp] electronic payment system went down in 17 states. This was apparently a glitch. I'm sure all of the talented Federale IT people are working in military intelligence, not EBT networking. In any case, the reactions at area supermarkets at this peak of subsidized shopping may give us a preview at what might happen if an entire subsidy cycle failed to feed the masses of massive misfits.

I donned my Ghetto Grocer apron [It is a cruddy threadbare old apron and I could use a replacement if any Third World sweatshop owners are feeling charitable.] and hurdled across the brownstone expanse of the Baltimore ghetto checking in on the beleaguered employees manning Fort Hoodrat and Cheap Guys R Us.

The Ghetto Grocer

At Fort Hoodrat there was much yelling about 'Da govoment not doin' shit'. The manager scrambled to make certain it was not his system that had gone down. Upon calling other grocers he discovered that it was a statewide meltdown. The ghetto customers dispersed, leaving behind about 40 loaded shopping carts to be re-shelved by the employees.

Those ghettoites in the know went across town to Cheap Guys R Us, a corporate chain store that has a policy of permitting a purchase of $150 per an order when the system goes down. The transaction is held for verification when the 'govoment' system goes back up. Since the system is down and no verification of funds is possible, hoodrat mammas who know well that they have no EBT funds remaining [or have not yet received theirs] will stop in for $150 in free food. These unredeemable transactions come to 10% of total. Cheap Guys R Us had 70 baskets of returns.

The most frightening thing about the Cheap Guys R Us version of the EBT Apocalypse preview was that the customers began to leave with loads of unpaid for food. There was one Harm City cop and one rent-a-cop on duty. Feeling overwhelmed by the mob of federally funded sumo-sized mammas the

Harm City cop called in for backup. I have no verfication on how many Harm City Store Troopers were required to stem the flood of gluttonous rebels and suppress a looting spree, as my source [105 pound Miss Ezz] was ducking for cover. I did, however, get a direct quote for a ghetto mamma battle cry; perhaps the same cry that shall ring out one day like the ejection of a car-sized pop tart from a skyscraper-sized toaster, "Yo don' dey know people gots ta eat!"

As a man recently commenting on the situation sagely noted, "It shows how close to the bottom things are."

Never fear, when that EBT airliner crash lands, the Ghetto Grocer will be there, braving hurled cheese curls and soda bottles, to bring you the story of the Rise of Militant Urban Obesity.

The Ghetto Grocer #6: What Retailers Do With The Meat You Eat, Part 1

© 2013 James LaFond

I'm proofing a novel and six novelettes this week, and trying to finish ghostwriting a book for another author before Christmas. So, when the clock strikes 10 A.M. I need to wrap this up.

That said there is a reason I'm writing this now, to out myself concerning a deception.

No, I'm not gay. Got you!

I have said often and written loudly that I resigned from my retail food manager gig in 2009 to go into 'reverse retirement' and devote the rest of my fading life to writing. I made this declaration in a partially seduced state, reflecting a particular bridge I did not burn, which would permit me to journey back across the river of damnation and take my place again among the management class.

The Ghetto Grocer

I was only able to pursue my writing goal with a clear conscience because I had left my youngest son with enough money to finish college. Recently I was reunited with a friend who I last saw soon after my resignation. She began asking me if I had stopped dating also. I told her, 'yes'. She then said, "You love kids so much I thought for sure you would have shipped a little brown girl over here and married her by now."

She knew me better than I thought she did. I had secretly harbored a possible return to the economy and the starting of a new family, if the writing thing went badly. I decided on this in the winter of 2011, six months after my resignation, after turning down the last of nine management offers. I had simply sought part-time work as a grunt.

While preparing my resume for a part-time job with a high end company, and knowing that I would be suspected of resigning under pressure, I prepared a paper called 'The Case Of The Hatfield Hams', this being one of the two reasons I resigned. The other reason—the tripwire—was the mistreatment of employees by my employer, which I dared not raise as law suits were pending. Six months ago I destroyed that document, lest I be tempted to post it in this space and forever cut myself off from my bread-winning capacity to support another disastrous mating decision. I now dredge it up from the bowels of my mind, forever insuring that I will never manage a retail food outlet again. The dates are graven into my mind and accurate down to the hour and minute.

Smoked Meats

Most abuses of meat products in retail food occur on 'the side wall' which is the highly profitable row of cases where a $10 an hour woman pushes as much money out the front door as the three male meat-cutters making $20 an hour do from the fresh meat case. I will relate one such story below. First you need to know about the government oversight, such as it is.

Municipal Health Inspectors

These are municipal employees who have their training geared toward policing restaurant kitchens. They know nothing about retail food. I managed a store with rampant abuses in the meat department, which I was not allowed to address, as Andy, the owner [a petite gay man who many

customers thought was my 'domestic partner'—
yuck!], insisted that he have direct control over the
meat room. Thus, when various disgruntled
employees and customers wanted to hit Andy
where it hurt by getting the store shut down for
health department violations, they called the local
health department and made complaints about the
meat department.

It fell to me to mislead these ladies without actually
lying to them. When they showed up at the desk
Andy would hide in the back office, call the meat
manager and tell him to get off the property, and
detail me or my co-manager, to 'run interference.' I
would stop by the executive restroom, fix my tie, do
my best Bill Clinton imitation in the mirror, "I did
not have sex with that cashier, Miss Laypinchski',
and "Well, it depends on what you definition of 'is'
is."

Now, having paid homage to my patron saint of
obfuscation I would approach the suspicious Harm
City health inspector and play, as my clerk Ty used
to say, "dumb-as-shit Jimmy! Boy, you lucky they
don't know how diabolic smart your evil ass is!"

The inspector would then take me to the section of
the case where the complaint had arisen, a section

of the case I had most likely policed the previous evening, removing the offending recycled meat. I will get into more details about this process in Part 3 when I deal with fresh meat. Suffice it to say that health inspectors have no idea how to tell if packaging and labels have been altered or tampered with. What they are good at is taking temperatures. So I would direct them to the thermostats, show them the case cleaning schedule signed my overnight janitor, and—if it was the Jamaican chick who wore the summer dresses—I would offer to walk her into the cooler. Islanders hate the cold. However, there is a government figure out there that you need to fear.

Department of Agriculture Inspectors

If you have a complaint about your grocer's meat case, call the Department of Agriculture. This is the best run agency of the U.S. Government: the only one that banks money for a rainy day, and operates WIC, which is the only sensible nutrition-based food subsidy program. These guys actually inspect this stuff at the plant, and know damn well if it has been tampered with when they see it at store level. When the Department of Agriculture Inspector came through that door I jettisoned my 'Slick Willy' template for my I-want-to-learn-at-your-knee-coach aspiring boxer mode. I never tried to bullshit one of these guys. Fortunately, of the hundreds of complaints we fielded, only 2 were handled by them. Mostly it was the health department fools.

The Case of the Hatfield Hams

On March 18, 2010 I was paged to the sidewall. A tall, blonde, angry, yuppie homesteader chick was fuming. As I approached with my Bill Clinton, I-love-the-world-and-you-too-baby-what-are-you-doing-tonight-sweetheart smile she pointed at the boneless 'football' hams and snarled, "I looked at these hams three days ago. They were dated for March Sixteenth. Now they're dated for April Twentieth!"

I bent to inspect the hams and she indicated a half-covered label dated for March 16, crudely covered with the new Aril 20 label. Her voice was shrill, "Is this what you do to oppress these poor uneducated people that don't know any better?"

I stood as tall as I could as she towered over me, "Miss, I do not do this. I can also tell you that my scumbag meat manager did not do this. You see, he would have used fingernail polish remover to remove any trace of the old sticker, just like he did with the Department of Agriculture seal which he removed using a cotton ball soaked in that noxious solution. Clearly, by the sloppy workmanship, this was Ricky's doing. I won't fire him, though I could, because I know the meat manager made him do it. I can't fire the meat manager because he is tight with the owner. I will remove these hams from the case—directly to the dumpster—otherwise they will end up back out here."

She was beside herself with frustration, and began to whine as women do when they have the ear of a man who they suspect understands and cares, "You mean to tell me this is going to continue? I can shop anywhere. But the local people, the elderly, the people that had to go to those terrible schools and can't read, and who don't drive, what about them?"

I was looking to get fired for good ethical reasons at this point so began to torch an old dry bridge in my life—the loyalty bridge. "Miss, the locals will call the health inspectors. I'll deflect their uneducated inquires and they will move on to the deli and write me up because I can't keep a hairnet on that platinum blonde back there. If I were you, I would call the Department of Agriculture. But, since my man Uncle Fester so thoughtfully removed the Department of Agriculture seal, it's not his business. Your only recourse will be the news: TV news."

She then became somewhat like a guilty post-orgasmic lover and sighed, "I don't want to put these people out of a job. I just want it fixed. Is there nothing you can do?"

I sighed to achieve empathy with my new partner in the battling of injustice, "Miss, I will write these men up—stack-up paper in their files. I'll detail one of my dry grocery guys—they can be trusted because I control their schedule and can reward them with overtime or time off—to sort this out every evening, as soon as Uncle Fester walks out the door."

She smiled, and then grinned, "Uncle Fester, seriously?"

"Absolutely Miss. I don't even know his real name anymore. He's seen managers come and go. I'll at least make his life hell until I go."

She smiled and shook my hand, "I'm so glad you're a good man. Thank you Sir."

"Thank you Miss."

I then stood and watched her walk away, me being in charge of safety and all. In case she took a misstep in those high heels I wanted to be right there to catch her.

Cracking the Hatfield Ham Code

I had Alex heave those hams in the dumpster as I filled out a write up, specifying each individual ham as a violation, as each had been weighed and priced separately. I would only issue a single write-up for a case of hot dogs packages for instance.

One copy for me.

One copy for Andy.

One copy for Uncle Fester or Ricky.

I then toured the entire case, and found other violations, amounting to 48, 48 each for the old-meat chief and his single sloppy Indian. Talk about writer's cramp. Andy was on vacation. I slid the stacked copies under his office door, which he always kept locked at all times to avoid suspicion, as that is where he had sex with his tall handsome boyfriend, who by-the-way, hated me.

I had an office clerk pull the meat orders from an Upstate New York wholesaler. My hunch was right. I discovered that the Hatfield hams in question, that had been dated for March 16, 2010, and then re-dated April 20, 2010, were just the tip of an unsavory meatberg. Those twenty or so hams were among the last of 420 hams that had gone out-of-date on September 24, 2009. They had had their seals removed in October, after being purchased from the packer, who had killed a few too many pigs for the pervious Easter it seemed. The hams had then been purchased by Andy and Uncle Fester on December 4 2009, to be sold for Christmas and New Years. These hams were now a year old, probably 14 months.

Uncle Fester's Ire

The next day I came into the meat room, armored in my ill-knotted tie, where Ricky was wrapping the chops that Uncle Fester was chopping. I handed Ricky his 48 write-ups and his eyes bugged out, "Jesus Jimmy!"

The Ghetto Grocer

I went and stood next to Uncle Fester, who glared at me out of the side of his eye while he continued chopping fresh pork, the meat—I reminded myself—that was most like human flesh. I said to Ricky, "Just listen to my reading to your boss, so I don't have to go hoarse reading this twice. You are both receiving the same notices."

I cleared my throat and Uncle Fester chunked a chop off with his 14 inch butcher knife against the stainless steel cutting table. Ricky took a step away. I preceded, "One Hatfield ham, Department of Agriculture seal removed—"

Ricky cut in, "But they came with the seals removed! They was already out-of-date!"

Uncle Fester looked at him with murder in his eyes and 'cachunked' a chop. Ricky flinched and stepped back. I decided to spice it with some feigned ignorance and sow disharmony among my rebellious underlings, "Thank you Ricky, I did not know that they were already out-of-date, until now."

Uncle Fester, reading my game, blocked my divide-and-conquer gambit, "I take full responsibility. I told him to date every ham."

"Of course, back to that. Falsely dated March Sixteen, re-dated April Twenty."

After reading each of the 48 write-ups I would place it down next to the bone saw by his side, and he would 'cachunk' a chop, with more vigor it seemed with every reading, even as Ricky shuffled a half step closer to the door. By the time I was done my reading there were far too many chops to sell that day, the edge of Uncle Fester's blade was dull, his face was purple, and Ricky was just about out the door.

I stepped out into the stockroom, put my back to the wall and began laughing my ass off. Ty was watching me with amusement and Ricky came out wringing his hands, "Jesus Jimmy! You almost ended up in the bone and fat can, and I would have had to clean up the goddamn mess!"

Ty, a goliath black man, walked away with a wide smile and howled to the ceiling, "Festerrrrrrrr!"

Epilogue

A month later I pulled Fester's file and saw that the write-ups had been destroyed. I was also unable to find the ham bill. Finally, on Sunday, July 4, 2010, at 5:57 P.M. my janitor, Alex, who looked like the mad scientist from the movie Back to the Future, and turned out to be the most conscientious perishable clerk in the building, came over to me with his dustpan in his hand, "Jimmy, Fester alert, Hatfield hams!"

I looked at him in disbelief, "Are you kidding me? We scoured the freezer for frozen hams months ago. Where the hell has he been keeping them?"

"Beats me Jimmy. Hell, the Nazis hid their V2s from Curtis Lemay. You never count out a tenacious foe. [Anyone who knows Alex knows I didn't make that dialogue up.] You better come here."

I followed Alex over to the smoked meat case and he pointed to a grayish football-shaped object. The ham had begun a full-on rot. Gases were escaping from the 18-month old re-formed pig flesh and causing the plastic wrapper to expand. Other, less fetid examples, resided in the bin beneath it, in less advanced stages of decay. Penning those seven write-ups for Uncle Fester was completed within the hour. At closing time at 7:05 P.M., I talked a violent drunk off the lot. He had been threatening customers who would not give him a three-pound bag of onions, as the store was already closed and he needed a three-pound bag of onions! I waited for the responding cop until 8:17, spoke with him, and never came back to work again, resigning 34 hours later in my street clothes.

To be continued in **Part 2: Running Over Hotdogs**

'How They Roll': The New Paradigm In Domestic Violence

© 2013 James LaFond

When I first arrived in Harm City over three decades ago, I was moving from a town near Pittsburg Pennsylvania where wife-beating and strangulation murder of women were, respectively, the leading types of assaults and murders. Upon arriving in this larger den of squalor I found murder to be predominantly male-on-male handgun. Where Baltimore gelled with Pittsburg was in wife-beating and domestic male-on-female abuse being the most common form of unarmed violence. Indeed, living in a working class environment, I can tell you that 10 of the 13 women I have dated in my life were either raped or beaten, or both, by husbands, boyfriends, uncles or fathers.

I have some good news to report. Men rarely beat women in Baltimore anymore. It happens, but is not even in the top three slices of the unarmed portion of the Baltimore violence pie. In my first week in Baltimore I saw a woman thrown from a jeep by a man while he was cruising at about 30 MPH. He then stopped, got out, pulled her up by the hair, punched her in the face, and dragged her back into the jeep and kept on trucking, slapping her all the while. That kind of stuff was common and cops could have cared less.

Now, in 2013, if your woman hits you, and you just grab her wrists and hug her while she screams, kicks and bites, you are still getting locked up! As pendulums do, this one has swung the other way.

As I write the three most common forms of violence against women are, from least to most common:

1. Unarmed mutual combat [fighting] with another woman

2. Muggings by loan black male youths, primarily for smart phones

3. Muggings by pairs of black youths, for the same

There is one new disturbing trend involving contract killings of women by male gang members at the behest of rival women.

The Ghetto Grocer

Also, another old standby is still with us, the murder of women by an estranged man who then takes his own life.

On the other side of the coin the most common form of violence faced by Harm City males are attacks by females: armed, unarmed, group, individual, straight, gay, hookers, cops, biker babes, black chicks, white chicks...

Permit me to illustrate a common occurrence from this morning, 11/12/2013, the sixth day of 'food stamps.' This account was had an hour ago from Miss Milge, who works at HoSmart FoodMart in West Baltimore.

"Oh baby, it was off the hook up in here! I was taking my choke break at parcel pickup and down by the cars is this food-stamper mamma screaming at her man. She rolled with a stream of cuss words: 'n-this,' 'm-effer that.' You name it. That's how they roll around here.

"He was your typical docile food-stamp-fed baby daddy, carrying the baby while she bought the shrimp, steaks, one-hundred dollar designer cakes and eighteen-dollar-a-pound crabmeat. He didn't say a thing. I don't know what he did, other than hold the baby and shield it while she beat him with her stainless steel cane!

"Oh, she beat his ass for a good ten minutes! That's no exaggeration, 'cause it took the assistant manager five minutes to get out there and the cops another five to roll up. There she was, whacking away and cussing up an n-word f-word storm the entire time. He must have some good legs. I can't believe he was able to stand up through that. You could hear it from fifty yards out: 'whack, crack, whack!'

"There had to be twenty cops there in ten minutes. They restrained her. It's a good thing the assistant manager [a white guy] was there, and spoke up for him, because they were going to arrest him. After he gave his statement the father was released and the mother was cuffed. That baby was nine months at best—could not walk yet, and there she was swinging a steel cane at the man that was holding that child. Imagine being that kid? What does she have to look forward to?"

No comment.

Plastic or Steel? The Harm City Return of the Shotgun Bandits

© 2013 James LaFond

Since late last month, deep in the bowels of Harm City, the Harm City Police Department has concentrated on breaking up the Black Gorilla Family. It is said this is because the Black Gorilla Family have been meeting in community parks, that they are in the sights of the FBI, and because they engage in crime as a matter of course. Others say that this attention is due to the fact that one of their incarcerated commanders arranged for the assassination of a male relative of Mayor O'Mamma, and that he impregnated four female corrections officers, thereby occupying—in a biblical way—a like number of Harm City PD 'gun racks'.

Just as a mid-summer sweep earlier this year against deep ghetto BGF territory drove violent criminals into surrounding communities, the latest anti-BGF initiatives have pushed violent crime into these same zones, which seem to be less heavily policed during major anti-BGF initiatives.

The most recent development, and the brilliant Harm City PD counterstroke, happened this week in my slice of the ghetto. Back in the early 1990s retail stickup artists who favored the shotgun were taking down supermarket cash rooms at a rate of two per week. Apparently their progeny has come of age. The dollar store I shop at was hit by shotgun-wielding bandits a few days back. The information I got from the shell-shocked cashier did not include the day, only that it was an early morning hit.

Knowing that my other shopping spot, Fort Hood Rat, would likely be next on the hit list if these guys were as unimaginative as their predecessors, I schlepped on down the road to speak with one of their security men. Surely the cops had approached him, had briefed him, had reminded him to report suspicious activity.

The cops had approached him shortly after the armed robbery up the street. They had something else in mind though. One of the dope-fiends, that he has become notorious for ejecting from the property, accused him of trafficking in bootleg

DVDs out of his car. That was enough for the cops, who arrested him on the job, leaving the store—which the police decline to protect in favor of the doughnut and coffee-dispensing convenience store down the street—temporarily unprotected.

There is no expectation that this unarmed security guard could do anything to thwart an armed robbery. He defends against lesser crimes and is charged with making sure his coworkers behave in the most survivable fashion, if it does come down to a robbery.

Here's to the upcoming winter in the ghetto.

Ghetto Grocer #7: Three Food Stamp Case Studies from October 2013

© 2013 James LaFond

Yesterday I stopped in to see Bubba [his real name] and asked him if he had any Ghetto Grocer news for me. He informed me that life behind the register had been uneventful this month, but that last month he had two extreme back-to-back food stamp customers. So, just in case you want to know what is being done with some of your tax dollars, here are two examples from either end of the very broad spectrum of people who are on the American version of the ancient Roman 'bread dole.' And we have something special sandwiched in between these two nightmare grocery orders.

"First, there is this black couple, an older man and his daughter, who has the card. They also have a number of WIC vouchers. They have a book with the pictures and descriptions of the products. I have the same booklet. Good to go. But no, he wants Cinnamon Toast Crunch. Can't have it. He wants it. He wants to argue about it. Five minutes that I'll never get back. Finally, they settle on something that is actually in the booklet.

"First off, they have this accent like they were living under the influence of some goofy-ass tribe. Off they go to get their thirty-six ounces of unsweetened cereal—shredded wheat I think. They're back with more 12 ounce boxes of sweetened cereal. I explained to them that the 18 ounce boxes of unsweetened cereal are clearly marked with green tags on the shelf. He then insists that they cannot get two 18 ounce boxes of cereal because that would exceed 36 ounces! They should issue a tazer with this job!

"I voided the check and they stormed out, griping about peanut butter or something.

"Then comes Miss Snow Bunny: skanky white chick with seven mixed kids, a five hundred dollar order and a thousand dollar balance, just skanking out kids for money. Three carts every time—fruit punch, cookies, chips, soda..."

"Right behind them comes this family: white, mom, dad, two girls—twelve maybe—and this bratty kid, ten I guess. They're well dressed. I ring out their order while the girls are hanging over the register saying, 'Don't mess up!', 'Don't make any mistakes!' 'You don't want to get fired!'

"Typical spoiled rich kids. The boy was quiet, looked like he tortured and killed small animals. These people are dressed well—thirty-five to forty. The order came to five-hundred-sixty-two and change. They have a fifteen-hundred dollar balance! There are some paper products that aren't stampable, so dad breaks out his money roll and peels off a twenty. He had to have a thousand dollars in that roll! The best part, was when I went out to rack their cart, which of course they were too lazy to rack, and I see them pulling off in the new black Escalade!"

"What can I say? That's America!"

Mo Coffee: Homeless in Harm City

© 2013 James LaFond

"I got a story ain't got no moral."

-Billy Preston

The Heartless Blogger

I was homeless for six weeks in 2003.

My new roommate Eric was homeless for about the same period earlier this year. [See Eric's Backpack below].

I have stepped over dozens of freezing homeless men, primarily in the late 1990s.

I have written 'The Case for The Panhandler Genocide.'

My column, 'Panhandler Nation' is largely a rant against the acquisitively homeless.

On the other hand I am a big fan of 17th Century pirates, Germanic nomad tribes, and Magyars, who were all essentially virulently covetous homeless folk.

So, what I am about to write may surprise you.

Beyond the Ghetto?

As a food market clerk, working for Good Guys R' Us out in the county, I pulled three shifts in a row leading up to Thanksgiving. I normally do not work even two nights in a row. This afforded me the opportunity to see a rare and melancholy drama unfold.

This slice of the suburbs, ten miles beyond the Harm City line, is no longer pristine; has become a ghetto annex, a target of slothful imminent domain. The postmodern ghetto is an ever-expanding phenomenon, hollowing out at its core to make way for urban homesteaders of the nearly wealthy class, even as the parasitic hood-rats scatter in pursuit of the receding civilization that is their reluctant host.

The Ghetto Grocer

Our store has been open for 24 hours since January. Doing this in the ghetto is suicidal on many levels, but is workable, here, far beyond the criminal epicenter of our society. The night captain discussed the eventual homeless encroachment of winter earlier this year, dreading the consequences and his inequitable role in the store policies that would surely ensue.

Mo Coffee

On Monday night 11/25/13 I noticed a black man in late middle-age, wearing slightly dirty sweats and old sneakers, limping through the store to the coffee pot. He is suffering from the onset of a nervous system disorder of some kind. He is very dark and has a droopy swollen lower lip. His appearance alone was enough to evoke pity. I have worked predominantly on majority black night crews throughout my life.

I have noticed that dark-skinned men with large lips are often ridiculed by their peers. Even the big dangerous ones get picked on behind their back, so you know it had to be bad for this guy in childhood. I once worked with a multiple murderer with the street name of Mumblejack. This dude was super scary. Even so, the other black clerks would make fun of him constantly with sayings such as, "Dat nigga straight from Africa!" and "Sheee, dat nigga got lips bigga den Mick Jagga!"

I found much to pity about this man, particularly the fact that he was on the street during a blast of cruel winter weather. I also found some things to admire.

He kept his purchases spread out to about one an hour and then took his time consuming them on the bench up front. When he no longer had a legitimate purpose to be in the store he would pace out front on the sidewalk, staying out of the way of customers, and even cleaning up trash.

He never panhandled.

When Charlene bought him coffee, he thanked her, and did not come back to her again expecting a handout. He even wiped the counter around the coffee pot. When other customers were nearby, he made himself scarce, not wanting to be a nuisance.

I took to calling him 'Mo Coffee' as he hit the pot every hour for the 13 hours I was on the job. He noticed when we would come up front on our breaks to sit, and would go outside during these times. This dude was the perfect homeless guy. On Tuesday night, as I took my seat on the bench to finish reading V.J. Waks novel Hammerspace on my break, Bubba, our cashier, nodded to Mo Coffee, and said, "You took his seat. He's going to stay outside in the cold until you're done."

Bubba came over and leaned on the back of the idle register lane, "He's a nice guy. It's kind of nice having him around. But you can see Reggie [the night captain] keeping an eye on him. How long do you think he'll be okay here?"

"He hit the jackpot. He is a low-impact specialist, the rare self-sufficient homeless guy. He has money. He spreads it out to make sure he's welcome or at least tolerated. He doesn't beg. He's a strong dignified man. Most of us would be crying in the gutter in his shoes, knocking on mom's door, begging for a space on the couch. He has survival protocols and sticks to them."

Bubba seemed surprised that I was not calling for his homeless head, knowing that I had once been among the cruelest and least tolerant store managers in the area. He nodded again, "So you think management will let him stay?"

"I would have bounced him out on Monday. I was a heat-seeking missile where loiterers were concerned. He's Daniel Boone—the polite pathfinder. We are the Indians. Management is the chiefs. The panhandlers, muggers and thieves that have chased him out of the ghetto, they are the white soldiers coming to rape and pillage. You have to kill the pathfinder or drive him off, or you get overwhelmed. Zero tolerance is the only defense. You can't solve the problem. You can just move it down the street. When I took that management job there was always a panhandler on duty, about a half-dozen a day. When I resigned there were none, but the Aldis down the street had a picket line out front. When the store was open for business every gap in the bars was covered by a dude I had bounced off my lot."

Bubba seemed sad, "Happy days."

"That's what Reggie is dealing with. He's already upset about telling this dude to get lost next week, when it's even colder out."

Bubba seemed to be weighing the social scheme of things, and whispered, with a long look at Mo Coffee, "I like having him around. He's a nice guy."

On Wednesday night, I asked Bubba, "Where's our man?"

"John [the store manager] put him out."

Bubba was noticeably depressed by the encroaching darkness of the world. I said what I could to assuage the 19-year-old, "At least he saved Reggie from the guilt."

Bubba nodded and said wistfully as we looked out into the icy night, "I hope he found a place, at least to eat Thanksgiving dinner."

"Amen brother."

'A Bigass Turkey': A Harm City Holiday

© 2013 James LaFond

The Ghost of this Thanksgiving past will not let me alone.

To be clear I have never been a Thanksgiving fan.

As a child Thanksgiving, and other such holidays, were primarily memorable for being occasions when my grandparents ignored me. These were normally the most attentive adults in my life, the ones that treated me more like an individual and less like a rank-holder in some disorganized organization.

As a teenager I began to suspect holidays were subversive efforts by the parents and teachers, who forever seemed to be in cahoots in their efforts to curtail my mind from losing focus upon their respective moneymaking and brainwashing obsessions.

As a father I dreaded holidays for it required me to referee squabbles and sniping bouts between the females of my family, over which of the competing matriarchs would have the honor of conducting the feast at her abode.

As a grunt grocer I liked Thanksgiving, as it was a paid day off. As a manager I dreaded it, for it meant a 22-hour shift, and reduced sales and increased expenses. [I know, that statement probably went more counter to your brainwashing than most of what came before it. In retail food Thanksgiving is nothing but an opportunity to lose business.]

I have come to regard Thanksgiving to be quintessentially American, or as American as propaganda can be without a war song. It is now, for me, as a writer, something to observe and comment on.

'I Wanna Bigass Turkey Bro'

Thus spake the transplanted Harm City whitetrashian, as I checked the dates on the refrigerated bagels. As I rose to guide him and his lady I noticed that they were both bombed out of their mind. They were East Baltimore by their accent. He was dressed in greasy jeans and denim jacket, and her in floral pajamas, yellow wife-beater, fuzzy bunny slippers, and a pink coat with a fur-lined hood.

We walked down the meat aisle, at 1:15 on Thanksgiving morning, toward the turkey section, occupied by three chicken-sized turkeys. As I stopped to point them out he pitched into me, and would have smacked face-first on the tile if I had not been in his way. He apologized and they began arguing about other stores they had been to. I eventually found them a huge frozen turkey that they might have been able to thaw out by Friday or Saturday.

They went up front to have Bubba check them out and discovered that they had forgotten her purse, and his wallet was empty. Out into the icy night they staggered, arguing all the way. Mind you, these were walk-in customers. They did not drive.

At 2:45 she was back, in her bare feet, her pajamas soaked up to her ankles, without a coat, and her face raw from the freezing wind. She was beginning to sober up. Apparently, her lord and master was unconscious by now. She stood proudly with a frozen turkey that was larger than her torso, tiny and emaciated as she was.

Her credit cards were denied.

She had nothing but change.

Her 'independence card' had $7.12 left on it.

As Bubba shook his head in dismay, knowing that this was not over, she turned to Nokia and I, where we sat on the bench taking our lunch. We were not laughing. She fairly cried, "This is not funny! I hate it out here! I hate the County. I want to live back in Highlandtown, but we can't! This is serious! I, will, be back for my turkey!"

Nokia and I watched her go, prancing out over the ice-covered asphalt. My female coworker gave me some chocolate [it was a KitKat, okay] and said, "That bitch don't have no shoes on her feet, en got no ride! You know she got kids at home if she got a card. Where her man?"

She gave me another KitKat and I answered, "Oh, he was in here earlier, drunk out of his mind. I suppose he's passed out at home. I have no idea what happened to her coat and bunny slippers."

Nokia looked at me in disbelief, "Is you serious, he laid up at home en she out in dis shit?"

I shrugged my shoulders in a teen-like 'I du-know', and she lit up, "Oh, hellll no! Sheeee. Dat bitch gotta be out a her mind!"

Fifteen minutes later, the lady returned with her payment, tears streaking her face, nose running, "I told you I'd get my turkey. This neighborhood sucks!"

As our validated heroine waddled off under the weight of the turkey into the dark cold of night, Nokia agreed, "I suppose it do suck if you a dumb barefoot bitch out on da street in da middle of da coldass night!"

A couple hours later about 20 neighborhood guys played a game of touch football on the lot waiting for the boss to hand out free pumpkin pies. They then came in and bought their whipped topping, grabbed a spoon from the deli, and ate out on the sidewalk. That is a nice local ritual that made me smile.

I then began considering all of the people I knew who had taken this holiday seriously this year, actually telling me what they were thankful for, and asking me what I was thankful for. This was off-putting as I thank people every day and could not recall anyone I had left out. Abstractly I suppose I am most thankful for not having ben born in South Sudan. Of the four folks who asked this question one was Mexican, one Brazilian, one Iranian, and one Russian. So much for my take on the 'quintessentially American holiday'. I know I'm not a very good America, but I mused, 'at least Thanksgiving hasn't been commercialized like Christmas'.

When I got back to work on Monday, after my four days off, which is what the holiday meant for me, I asked a Christian coworker how her holiday had been. She said, "My daughters had to have dinner wrapped up in the afternoon so we could be at WalMart before six, when they cut the plastic on the pallets. It was like a feeding frenzy; wall-to-wall people. Do people even eat Thanksgiving dinner anymore?"

That made me feel better for Mister and Mrs. Bigass Turkey, who may have enjoyed their version of a holiday meal as early as Friday, when the savage worshippers of our Supreme God were flooding his temples in their many millions.

'Dirty Thirty' The Ghetto Grocer #8: War Stories from a Washington D.C. Area Grocer

© 2013 James LaFond

Yesterday I was reminiscing about the grocery business with 'Travolta', an old friend who did a few tours in Washington D.C. area Giant Food stores. Below are some soiled memories of his.

Jack

Travolta began back in 1979, in a store that was not too terrible, and worked with a traumatized Vietnam Vet I will call Jack. Jack was a famously anti-management union guy in an industry where the unions sold out to management a long time ago. He had been a tunnel rat, and people feared him. He once killed and ate a crawling insect while a manager was speaking to him—end of conversation. Once, when a customer asked him for a firmer head of cabbage, he wrapped a coconut in cabbage leaves and gave her that, twirled up in a plastic bag.

On another occasion management—who liked giving him dirty jobs and sending him to work in the worst stores—directed him to deliver a dozen roses to an address, without first inquiring the nature of his vehicle. It was a motorcycle of course. He placed the first rose in his mouth, drove across town, delivered the rose, and returned to the store for the next rose. On it continued in this fashion until he had delivered all 12 roses.

"We worked together in produce, so naturally spoke with one another often. On discovering that I had some intelligence, he said, 'Travolta never let management know how smart you are or they will make your life hell.' How right he was about the cutthroat character of retail food management."

Langley Park

"Good God, what a place! It was surrounded by the dregs of the world: poor Koreans, poor Russians, poor blacks, poor Jews. A supermarket reflects the neighborhood. You go to an upscale supermarket, it is wonderful. You go into a low income store, God help you. We were in a shopping center that had a K-Mart. If you want to know what it was like back then listen to the song 'Christmas in K-Mart' by Root Boy Slim.

"My first day there the security guard tackles a shoplifter, puts him in an arm lock, and says, "Stop, or I'm gonna break it. He repeats this. The shoplifter continues to struggle, and he snaps the arm. You could hear it pop! Then he handcuffs the shoplifter to the railing in the doorway until the cops get there. In the meantime customers are navigating their carts around this shoplifter with the broken arm.

"I'm working on the night crew. It is three a.m., when these three heroin addicts come in and start raking stuff off the shelves—just trashing the place! The security guard is unarmed. The night captain runs for the phone outside the courtesy booth to call the police. One of the addicts throws a glass jar of citrus slices at him and shatters the phone. One addict begins yelling that he is going to go to his car and get a gun and kill everyone. Eventually the police got there to arrest two of them—the other having disappeared I think. In the meantime the security guard grabbed a fire extinguisher and beat one of them senseless with it. The cops told us later that one of the addicts had a gangrenous foot that had to be amputated at the hospital. Just disgusting!"

Dirty Thirty

"Store Thirty was the worst. We called it Dirty Thirty. I got transferred there and I notice I'm driving past this street where someone is found shot to death on the news daily. One day there was a flaming Mercedes Benz on the lot! The security personnel were armed. The first thing they would do when they came in was strip down their pistols and load them! The neighborhood was so bad the store was not open twenty-four hours, and they still had an armed guard in the store at night!

"You know how they have manager trainees, for the front end. We had this new manager trainee who was left in charge on a slow night, to get that crucial practice closing down a store after business. This customer comes up front that night and approaches her at the courtesy, telling her that she should check the men's room. She walks back to the men's room. Mind you, this is in a food store, and this is where the employees sanitize their hands for work before they handle your food.

"There is a man shaving at the sink.

"Another man is taking a dump.

"And, between those two is a jon, who has this prostitute bent over and is ass-fucking her!

"She walked up front, set her keys down, and walked out, never to be seen again."

Mamma, don't let your babies grow up to be retail food clerks.

Ghetto Grocer #9: What Retailers Do With the Meat You Eat: Part 2, Running Over Hotdogs

© 2013 James LaFond

In the mid 1980s I was a night crew member in a Harm City supermarket. My Friend, Ronbone, was the assistant manager responsible for closing the store at night. As I worked perishable grocery and did the store audit [checking dates on shelf product, and pulling what was out of date] he often consulted with me concerning the meat case. This particular meat case was run by 'Rancid Ray' a notorious purveyor of past-dated product. The following story touches on some of the techniques used to 'rework' out of date smoked meat products.

The Case of the Memorial Day Hotdogs

The manufacturer of the above named hotdogs is a local Baltimore area packer, who shall remain nameless, as they truly were blameless in this case. The astonishing thing about the habit of some meat managers pushing out of date smoked meat products is that the packer will buy it back. But, 'Rancid Ray' was never one to take a packer's wholesale buy-back when he could get the customer's retail purchase, especially when he purchased the item for a sale price, and wanted to slack it out at regular price and 'whore up the margin'.

'Rancid Ray' bought in his memorial day hotdogs at the end of April, a month before the holiday, so he could get them at the packer's end-of-winter closeout price, as they were shedding their old inventory to make way for the making of the hotdogs that were in fact intended to be sold for Memorial Day consumption. That year, I believe Memorial Day fell on a 24th or 25th. The hotdogs went out of date on the 29th. Needless to say, Ray's sales were not what he expected, as most of our customers had automobiles, and therefore the ability to drive to the local chain store and buy fresher hotdogs. One night after Memorial Day Ronbone took me into the meat room and pointed to a pallet of hotdogs that had just gone out of date, and said, "What the hell is he going to do with that?"

I responded, "I don't think you want to know."

Manicured Dogs

It had been well established that the Rancid One loaded his case with reworks in the early evening after his more upstanding first cutter went home. Friday night was a big night for him to push old product as this was back in the day when Friday evening and Saturday morning were peak food purchase times. Now it is Saturday afternoon and late Sunday morning.

The next Friday night Ronbone pointed out a display of these hotdogs—hundreds of packages—which were all dated with an ink stamp for July 5th. He asked me, "Okay, you're the evil mastermind. Where did he get plant-dated hot dogs? Did they just send him new wrappers or what?"

I informed Ronbone that that would be something a packer would never do, and that Rancid Ray lacked the vacuum-sealing equipment to achieve the customer comforting seal.

Consumer Note: Never purchase a package of refrigerated foods in which the vacuum seal is broken, indicated by air pockets between the wrapper and the product.

We took a trip back into Rancid Ray's devil's workshop, the piled boxes of nic-nacs and ad circulars above the rewrap table, a table, that, in my opinion, should not exist.

Having brought a package of hotdogs with us I cracked open a sealed case and retrieved one pack, and then a half empty case, and retrieved one from there. The original May 29th date on the package from the sealed case was stamped in fine ink. The hotdog package from the display had a wide and somewhat smudged ink. The package from the open case had no date!

I rooted through Ray's box of secrets and found a half-empty bottle of fingernail polish remover, held it up, and snarked, "What are the chances that Ray is a transvestite?"

Ronbone was in awe of Ray's evil genius as I then produced Mister Tony's old ink stamper that he had used to price frozen orange juice back in the days before scanning.

Ronbone had me pull the case, and we sat the hotdogs on the cutting table. The next morning I heard screamed obscenities from back in the meat room not long after Ray arrived. Before I left at 8 a.m. he had the hotdog display loaded, having spitefully re-dated the hotdogs to July 6th! And so it went, twice a week we pulled the hotdogs, and twice a week he re-dated them a day ahead, until the hotdogs being put out were a fresh looking July 29th. This war went on below the ownership horizon, as both Ronbone and Ray doubted the owner would back them; Ray being a senior big-earning department manager, and, Ronbone, while having right on his side, being the youngest member of the management team.

The March of the Immortal Dogs

By the end of June, as the hotdog pallet continued to diminish, the dates on the packages on display continued to advance into the future toward Labor Day, as they would have if they were freshly purchased shipments being rotated into the case. You see, Rancid Ray's genius was to avoid making it look like he just had one big mess of hotdogs bought in at the same time. His dating scheme assured that it would seem to the customers that he was bringing in fresh product twice per week.

The Pact

Ronbone brought this process to the owner, who confronted Ray, who lied through his teeth. Believing Ray's vehement assertions that Ronbone was smoking too much pot, and should mind the front end and not the meat case, the owner reprimanded Ronbone. Ronbone was a big nasty dude, who beat his girlfriend and did more drugs than Jimmy Hendrix and Jim Morrison combined. But he had a soft spot for the many senior citizens in the neighborhood who shopped with us, and did, despite his depravities, believe in right and a wrong. He said to me, with tears in his eyes [for Ray's sins were many and extended far beyond hotdogs], "These are my friends. These old people could die from food poisoning. What do we do?"

"Well, we can't be seen taking anything out of the building to the dumpster—that's our ass. We can render the stuff unsalable, if you have the balls to stand up to Mister... when he comes after you."

Ronbone, was not a bad conspirator. He put his hotdog size finger to his chin and said, "Ray thinks he dodged a bullet. He'll just try and out do us— won't go to Mister..."

We shook hands, and Ronbone rumbled, "It's on Jimmy. It's on!"

The Strategic Hotdog Command

We had his production facility and methods down. We just had to time our strikes appropriately. It was now late July/early August, and the immortal dogs kept marching into the limitless future, the pallet in the meat box slowly melting down to the last 25 cases or so. Then came our watershed event.

One Friday night Ronbone had been inspecting the ever refreshed hotdog display, of dogs that were now about 4 months old, and had been out of date for over 2 months, but nevertheless grew new legs and continued to march to the checkout lane. The factory vacuum seals, were, however, beginning to fail. We went with this phenomenon and replicated it, by popping the seals with our hands, and tossing all of the compromised packages into the back. Every time Ray loaded the case with 'fresh' dogs, now being dated for September 9th, to be sold through Labor Day, we would pop the seals and set them in the back.

As we closed in on the end of August we popped what had to be the last seals. Then, the next night, we noticed a new brand of hotdog in the case, displayed in Styrofoam meat trays overwrapped on the machine used to wrap steaks and such. They were labeled, 'Ray's Fresh Hotdogs.'

Ronbone looked at me and hissed, "The meat box!"

With that we rushed back into the meat room and then into the box, to find that the pallet of vacuum-seal compromised dogs was still there, repacked in the boxes, from where they were being plucked and then transformed into 'Ray's Fresh Hotdogs.'

Ronbone looked at me and asked, "What can we do?"

I examined the pallet and noticed that Ray was doing this work in stages, and announced, "We have to hit him in the production phase. He doesn't have all day for this. He has to cut meat too."

Ronbone and I took the newly packaged dogs and threw them in the 'bone and fat' cans, which were not kept under refrigeration necessary for food stored for human consumption. Surely he would not reuse those dogs.

Hotdog Armageddon

The next day we came in and found that the 'shit-canned' dogs had been displayed. Ronbone went into a rage, took the dogs in the back, and cut them in half with a butcher knife, throwing them in the bone and fat can. He stood and breathed heavily to calm himself, and rumbled, "It's on now!"

A few nights later, perhaps a week out from the Labor Day weekend, Ronbone awaited me by the meat case, a dejected downcast look distorting his face as he leaned against the case housing. I came up to him and he walked me solemnly over to the prominent cutout in the meat case where Ray now proudly displayed his 'Ray's Fresh Hotdogs.' Ronbone pointed to a new item in Ray's selection, an array of economy-sized packages of hotdog slices, labeled 'Ray's Fresh Hotdogs for Beans'!

We both broke into laughter, which turned to tears, having been bested by a true artist. Finally Ronbone looked down at me, and grumbled, "What can we do against this guy—he's a fucking God!"

"I got it. Grab them and bring them back to the stockroom. I'll get his wrapped and un-priced case. We can still interdict his production."

Ronbone and I met in the stockroom with his box full of pulled dogs for beans and Ray's case of wrapped 'fresh' dogs to be priced up and displayed in the morning. I dragged out the 1-ton forklift, and placed the case and box of dogs on the concrete floor between the forklift and the stack of empty pallets it had been parked under.

Ronbone stood back to the side, and I leaned on the control arm of the stand-behind lift and said, "The wholesaler doesn't let us send back mislabels. So when I order green beans and they ship me goose liver pate in a tin, or Armour tripe in milk gravy, I send it back as damaged! They give us credit for damage, and this is how we damage it, the same way they do at the warehouse, with a forklift!"

I then cranked the lift up to its maximum speed of 5 MPH and speared both cases, lifted them, and then ran the giant twin shish kabobs into the stack of pallets, smashing the dogs between the 17 pallets pressed against the stockroom wall and the steel uprights behind the forks. Ronbone hollered with joy as I speared, and mashed, and smashed, and finally even ran over the hotdogs. It was an orgy of meaty destruction, two defiant clerks in their early twenties striking back at the corrupt world of retail food in the name of the elderly patrons who were loath to abandon their neighborhood market for the chain store out the road.

We placed those two boxes of mashed hotdogs on the re-wrap table, shook hands, and went our separate way with a feeling of victory.

The next night, Ronbone intercepted me at the door, grabbed me by the shoulder and walked me over to the case. He did not even have to point at the slice of contentious display space that we had fought over heroically for the past three months. There were two new items in the case. Alongside 'Ray's Fresh Hotdogs', and 'Ray's Fresh Hotdogs for Beans', were 'Ray's Diced Hotdogs for Spaghettios', and 'Ray's Fresh Bologna Salad!'

Ronbone put his hands in his slacks pockets and shook his head, mumbling, "The man is an artiste. We can't stop him, can we?"

I reached up and patted the big man on the back with a conciliatory tone, "We're all out of bullets and he's got plenty more Indians."

He turned and shook my hand, and said, "Thanks for the help. I actually thought I could be a manager. What a joke. It's just spitting in the wind."

Afterward

Some 20 years later I would return to this store as a grizzled old veteran of shift work and special assignments in 34 stores, and take the General Manager position. Rancid Ray was still there, up to his old tricks, and on my hit list. In 2006 I would take up Ronbone's lost cause. Would I fare any better?

Find out in **What Retailers Do With the Meat You Eat: Part 3, Frying Ray's Bacon.**

Ajay and The Fool: A Ghetto Grocer Snap Shot

© 2014 James LaFond

Residents of Harm City know that the cheapest and safest place to purchase your bootleg DVDs is at the local Nubian hair salon. As these ladies make their monthly visit to drop a week's pay on their hair do, they are accustomed to street venders coming in to sell stolen goods and bootleg movies. Batteries, buttafinga candy bars, and Dove bar soap are three high demand items. Fresh food though, is rarely sold to women who are having their hair treated, cut, weaved, ejection molded, and what have you.

This past Sunday Ajay, an unlikely NASCAR fan and heavy metal concertgoer, was having her hair done. I'll let her tell it:

"I was sitting with my hair under the [I missed this word, for whatever otherworldly device bakes hair while still on the head] while Michelle was doing something when this man came in. He was older and had a bag. He walked over to Michelle and tapped her on the arm. She ignored him. Well, I suppose this was not clear enough for this trifling fool so he tapped her again. She ignored him. Then he came over to me and grabbed my wrist! Boy! You best not be coming into a salon and touching people in the chair!

"I grabbed his wrist and threw it off. He was weak, a weak, stupid, trifling fool. Then he was like, 'Come on baby, don't you wanna buy some meat?' and he was holding up this shopping bag full of God knows what kind of stolen mishandled meat that nobody in their right mind would ever buy—especially where hair is being done.

"Oh, he left alright."

Ajay was duly horrified when I informed her that shoplifted meat is routinely sold in Harm City bars, and even on busses, and at bus stops. I sometimes go to one bar, at which the owner's permit a pair of thieves—a husband and wife couple—to keep a folding table behind the stairs. On Saturday night, at 11:00 p.m., the man hauls in a backpack and two wheeled coolers as the lady sets up the table and begins arranging the display and announcing prices of $2, $5, and $10 dollars, on high retail items like meat, Tide, club pack candy, etc. Once this Bonnie and Clyde team of shoplifters set up their display

The Ghetto Grocer

and announce prices, if some patrons hold back
from shopping, they proudly announce that they
only sell items stolen from Walmart. That breaks
the ice and everyone rushes the table. Then, after
everything is sold—which takes about 20
minutes—the little lady takes next week's orders
on a memo pad. I am the only patron at this bar
who does not shop with the Walmart resellers.

Your Momma Does Not Work Here: A Ghetto Grocer Snapshot

© 2014 James LaFond

A friend of mine who works as a janitor at a high end gourmet supermarket in a rarified suburban enclave called me on Saturday night to complain about a 450 pound male employee that works in the deli and does not wash his hands, or anything else it seems. Teddy, the janitor in question, has to clean up after this man in the men's room using a degreaser on the toilet seat. He then texted me the contents of a sign that the owner has recently posted in the lunch room:

Your momma does not work here.

Clean up after yourself!

You might live like this at home, but it's not acceptable at work.

Put your trash in the trash can that's sitting inches from the table, and wipe your mess up.

Failure to maintain a clean eating area for yourself and others will result in the removal of the picnic table.

No one wants to eat on top of your trash!

And you're attracting bugs and mice.

Trifling

The employees that use this lunch room might be putting together your party platter.

Walmart's Most Wanted: A Ghetto Grocer Epilogue

© 2014 James LaFond

In Ghetto Grocer #4 we sang the song of Scabby Abby, the supermarket bakery clerk, who did not wash her hands, threw her underwear away in the restroom after—well, after, brushed her teeth in the hand sanitizing sink, applied Fixodent to her dentures on the bakery prep table, tested her sugar levels there too, scratched her heroin sores over the bread slicer, licked her fingers while she iced cup cakes, and defecated in the backyard of a Baltimore country family home while waiting for the bus.

Really, you threw that doughnut in the trash? But it looked so good! Perhaps we could arrange a wedding between Scabby Abby and Denizen Cane.

People in the retail food business migrate from company to company. I am often called by managers for references and clerks for tips on dealing with the managers. Just last night two informants from my ghetto grocer intelligence network came through for me concerning the fate of Scabby Abby at her new workplace—Walmart!

Both informants told me that Scabby Abby was firing up heroin in the Walmart restroom while on the clock. She even had her arm tied off. Although the Scabby One claimed to be giving herself insulin, she was not believed, and was fired and barred from the premises.

Not only was this outcome tragic in that Abby no longer has access to a full service restroom. But, according to my female source, Scabby Abby's photo [which will generally be taken of a shoplifter and placed on a 'barred board' in the security office] was posted at each register, facing the customers, with the caption, "Do not hire this person"!

Conservative Cashier to be Martyred by Retailer: A Ghetto Grocer Reality Check

© 2014 James LaFond

Karab Amabo & Herod's Men

Just this morning I found out through the godless media voice of CNN that Omaha Nebraska police have wrongly abducted and videoed the future President of the United States flipping them off and cussing them out. What else is a diapered dude supposed to do when Five-O kicks in yo door before the Honey Nut Cheerios be done? They then compounded their atrocity by unjustly labeling him a 'thug toddler', uploading the video to YouTube and taking him from the custody of the future Mother Dowager of our great empire.

With stuff like this going on I'm prepared to believe anything. Then, I got a call a scant hour ago on the Ghetto Grocer Hotline from an embattled ghetto cashier who has just experienced the following.

The Ghetto Grocer

Tashika & The Trannys

The day before yesterday, in a major supermarket, operated by a national retailer, Tashika [a black female liberal democrat] was manning her register when three black male transvestites came to her line. They each set what might, or might not have been, separate orders on her belt. Then the lead tranny walked away. Wondering if she should begin ringing out the order as one, or as three separate purchases, Tashika pointed to the cross-dressing man and said to his friends, "Is he goin' ta pay for that?"

The three men then began to howl with disapproval over her discriminating against the hairy-legged male in the miniskirt by referring to him as a 'he'. He was 'as much a bitch as her', and would not be denied his identity. A protracted scene ensued as management and even law enforcement was called to deal with this violation of hermaphroditic rights!

Finally, the episode entered its most bizarre stage when the store manager [a white male conservative republican] confronted Tashika—an unlikely martyr for the neo-conservative cause if ever there was one. He said, "Tashika, why did you have to call her a he?"

In keeping with her belief in clear gender identification, just like Perpetua before the leopard in the arena, she stood her ground, "Because that is obviously a dude!"

The diplomatic manager continued, "Couldn't you have at least apologized?"

Although I am not certain that her head bobbed horizontally above her shoulders, one may be forgiven for assuming that it did just that as she said, "What, for not bein' blind?"

All I know at this point is that 'corporate' is attempting to deflect a lawsuit, most likely via recourse to the venerable retail food tradition of, 'Throwin' her ass under the bus!'

I have no comment, other than to once again note that I am serenely pleased that I am no longer standing in her manager's shoes.

Heinous Huffers: The Most Despicable Dopefiends

© 2014 James LaFond

Last Wednesday night during the recent blizzard I made it to work at Fred's Fine Foods For Foodstampers just before midnight. I work the frozen foods and dairy case over night. The place was trashed. What was glaringly apparent was that the whipped topping section in the dairy was empty. There were only a few cans left. The night captain was walking by and I pointed at the empty shelf, "Do we have a surge in bachelorette parties around here."

He shook his head in disgust and set down three cans of the aerosol dairy cream and groused, "The drug dealers must be snowed in. All of the druggies are walking out with this stuff."

An hour later after I stocked the section two snot-nosed punks, pasty white and pimpled, and doing a piss poor job of representing the Caucasian gene pool, came through the aisle and headed back to the bathroom. While I was stacking my empty pallets these two headed up front. A minute later Ron came back with an armful of Readywhip and handed it to me, "I told the dummies if they didn't cough it up I was calling the police, so I didn't have to chase them. As stupid as they are the last thing they need is to be snorting more of this stuff."

Huffing aerosol is predominantly a passion of white teenagers, although, in later years many will fall back on it in lean times long after they have moved on to better drugs. When I worked in South Baltimore I had to check the aerosol whip before I touched it. Down there those fends would unzip the seal and blast all of the gas up their nose right there in the aisle, resulting in nose bleeds. Most nights that I worked at the Fort Avenue store I had at least one canister on the dairy shelf with blood and other nasal secretions dripping down the side.

This was also a habit in Northeast Baltimore stores. I once worked with a crew who all huffed the Airwick room freshener and then sat back against the pallet stack and giggled and said "Wow man" for an hour.

South Baltimore was the worst. There were three particular boys who had stomped an older black dishwasher to death a month before I began working in the neighborhood. My new coworkers told me to be careful walking on Key Highway coming in because these guys were notorious, their Uncle was politically connected, and everyone in the area 'knew' they had killed the man, but they had not even been arrested. I thought the stories of the murder seemed a bit over blown, and did not imagine the cops being that incompetent.

Then one night, while I was stocking the ice cream with my back to the Readywhip case, these three came in behind me and starting huffing gas. When the security guard said something to them they started bragging about having beaten a man to death. If I said anything it would have ended badly. The lead kid was short and potbellied. I turned to put my plastic in the trash box and accidently shoulder butted him in the chin. They all got quiet while I stared in his face. I was holding a large utility knife in my right hand. I told the security man that I needed to get a cart from out front and would be walking up with him. The three punks walked between us chuckling, mumbling and acting tough, until they got to the checkout. The security guard put the canisters on the belt so they could pay for their huff, and out the door they went, without a fuss.

I hope one night I get to see one of these fiends literally blow his brains out with this stuff. I'll gladly swing the mop that erases his stain.

Fort Hoodrat Blues: The Day Before Food Stamps In An Embattled Ghetto Food Market

© 2014 James LaFond

Last Wednesday March 5th, was a somber day in the hood.

The last shot of food stamp EBT money had come out way back on February 16th.

By the 16th every junky bitch is bone dry, having traded their stamps for dope day one.

By the 20th every baby's mama is out of stamp money, their monthly diet cycle shifting from pork chops and steamed shrimp to beef-heart and chicken-part hot dogs and ramen noodles.

By the 27th even the drug dealers are out of stamps, having laid in party grub and sodas by the case.

Come the 1st the only money on the streets is in the hands of dope friends who still live with aged parents or grandparents whom they defraud of their SSI at the ghetto-mart bill pay window.

By the 5th, food market employees are starving themselves, on minimal hours, even as the hoodrats scrounge for backwash bottles, cigarette butts, and the ridges of milk chocolate left adhering to the wrapper of a hastily consumed peanut butter cup.

The scene is set at Fort Hoodrat, embattled Harm City EBT Mecca, where a skeleton crew labors away for Mister Stampenstien.

Enter Journee

8:15 am

Journee is short, pregnantly round, and maternally proud; an object of racial oppression, economic recession and entitlement-fueled aggression, with but three dollars to her name.

Journee stepped back to the deli counter and sees but one woman behind the counter. She calls over the shoulder of the elderly man before her, "Yo, are you the only bitch back here?"

The Ghetto Grocer

The woman behind the counter responds, "I'm the only bitch that's gonna wait on you!"

The old man moves on, and Journee demands a sample of honey ham, which she eats, finding it not up to her standards of sweetness. She then demands a sample of spiced ham, which she eats, finding it too spicy. She then demands a sample of pickle loaf which she eats, declaring it too salty. Journee then calls for a sample of smoked turkey, which she eats, declaring it too smoky.

The rude white bitch behind the counter than says, "Look hon, I'm about ta give you two slices of bread and charge you for a sandwich!"

Journee takes offense and reaches into her bag of oratory—somehow forgetting the 21 Loeb translations of Cicero she read—and blurts, "Fuck you!"

The deli clerk then counters, "No, fuck you! I work for my money. Shit, I work for your money! You're my dependent [and rudely pointing to the sainted fetus in waiting] and you're about to pop out another parasite!"

The Ghetto Grocer

Journee—cussing all the while, demands a quarter pound of bologna from the 'white bitch' behind the counter—sliced extra goddamn fuckin' thin—and walks away in a huff.

Journee notices the white bitch behind the bakery counter grinning and says, "Fuck you too bitch" and continues up front to grab herself that 'cheap-ass OJ dat be on sale'.

When she gets to the OJ case by the courtesy office she notices that 'that dyke-ass white bitch' has not got it stocked, and speaks over the shoulder of an elderly sista to the white bitch behind the counter, "Where dat cheap-ass OJ dat be on sale?"

The courtesy bitch responded, "It's being unloaded off the truck right now. It will be a while. She's on the dock with the order."

Journee responds, "Dat's not the ansa I wanted ta hear!"

The courtesy bitch then says, "Sorry miss."

Journee then goes off, "Fuck you, you ghetto-ass white bitch!"

The Ghetto Grocer

She then stepped over into Roland's register lane, and made common cause with the young brutha, "Dare a ghetto-ass white bitch in da deli, a ghetto-ass white bitch in da bakery, en dis ghetto-ass white bitch up in hea!"

Roland leans back with his hands spread wide and says, "Really? Really! Over a dollar OJ. Come on; is you serious?"

Journee throws the bologna on the belt and barks, "Fuck you too!" and righteously walks out the door, leaving Roland behind dismayed, "I don't need this shit. I got my pregnant wife yelling at me all day every day."

This story was based on interviews with two of the heartless employees who failed in their mission to separate Journee from her last three dollars, which walked out the door in her hand, having come oh so close to leaping into Mister Stampenstein's bank account.

'Da Complexion Fo Da Protection': Working The Tie Shtick As a For-profit Shoplifter

© 2014 James LaFond

Last Wednesday, the day before food stamps hit, a grungy stolen food vendor walked in with a grocery store manager. The retail food management uniform is basically dark slacks, white dress shirt, and tucked in tie. I'm looking at a carbon copy of the late 40s retail food tyrant I once was, walking in non-gay partnership with a scrounge ball skinhead food fence of the type my co-manager and I used to tackle on the parking lot.

They avoided me like the plague while I glare at them and considered calling Duz on the phone so he could drive over here and beat their asses by the pool tables while I pounded back a cheap beer.

Duz is a famous Baltimorean hard ass. [In The Logic of Force he is pictured in the shirt that says 'Shuck me, suck me, eat me raw'.] He was once run over with 20 K in cash under his arm by a Buick while the thug on foot with the gun lost ground in the foot chase. The would be getaway car was totaled and the cash caught up in the wheel well. Duz trained with me that night, his big polish ass immune to automotive assault.

One time three Baltimore City pigs came into the store flashing badges and demanded that he cash a fourth party check. He answered, "No." The pigs waited for him to get off work and followed him to the bar. They bought him beer, after beer, after beer, trying to get his block-head protected brain pickled, not realizing that immunity to alcohol was one of his superpowers. When the bar closed, with Duz a case deep into their pork pay, they followed him outside to make a DWI arrest, and he waived them off, "Thanks for the brewskies, I'm walkin'. You can follow if you like." [He had a pit/boxer mix named Chico who ate cats whole and was trained to attack anyone but me, Corky, and babes on sight].

But Duz really came into his own when it came to thieves who sold in bars. One night we were drinking tequila with two babes when he said, "Go look in the freezer."

I was shocked to discover $100 worth of steak from a competitor. He explained to me that he was slamming back brews at the Pub when some 'low life' came in selling our steaks. Well, he actually robbed the guy in front of the bar tender and patrons; taking his money, the packs of Walmart underwear, and the steaks. He chuckled as we got into his hot tub with the floatation devices of the night, "I was so drunk I couldn't even read the label. Go figure. You're the philosopher. Does that make me a thief?"

"It makes you just in a world without justice, a vigilante."

He then toasted me, "With steaks on the grill!"

Well, I decided not to call in a Duz strike on the suit and the trash and just took out my notepad. After they left I asked their customer, Reggie, who 'placed an order' with the men before they left, "What's up with the store manager? You mean to say he's in on it too? He must be the CSM or Co. The top guy makes too much for this shit, even if he's on coke."

Reggie said, "Nah, Nah ma man. Listen to me. I don't mean ta be racist. Da fact is, he got da complexion fo da protection!"

I got it immediately. "He's impersonating the new district manager, coming through on inspection.

The staff runs and hides from these dudes, and the store managers have off on Wednesday, and he [the manager] is the only company employee—the only person at store level—who really even knows who works out of the district office! He's even got the standard bad pasted comb-over."

Reggie, apparently pleased to meet a streetwise and management wise man, said, "Ya see you gotz the complexion fo da protection—could work dat shit yo own self!"

And so it goes, in the ghetto.

Merely Reprehensible: Zombie Bait #3

© 2014 James LaFond

This morning, out in Harm County, where the white buffalo roam in their Dodge Ram 4-by-4's, I was finishing up the frozen food case for Mister John, at Free Food For Fat F...s, when **he** entered'; a man with no name; a man worthy of no name; a sign of the times; a tic on the body politic.

I know that all of you liberals assume he is a handicapped ghetto kid, who, if you put Johnny Knoxville in charge of testing at an Ivy League school, might be able to gain admittance.

Of course you conservatives think he is a milk-sucking stay-at-home liberal dad.

Yes, and you MANLY 'manosphere' MEN are certain that he must be a she, or at least a he-she, at best a feminist.

The Ghetto Grocer

You libertarians are certain that he is a government employee, like all of the cops that pay for their groceries with food stamps in Baltimore.

And you alternative right guys—and you, you loan alternative right babe—are certain that he is an illegal alien; probably some godforsaken 'mud-person' from south of the border, come here to take from you what your great, great, great, great worked-to-death grand daddy's master took from some Stone Age holdover with a feather in his hair and a tear rolling over his cheek...

But really, who is this man with no name, this Clint Eastwood of State subsidized groceries?

The answer is: he is merely reprehensible. I began the Zombie Bait series so that those purely parasitical proto-hominid effluvia deposits on the body economic would not be elevated to the level of such Streets Have Eyes characters as Denizen Cane, Bruce the Bricklayer, Newnetthelove, Jervis the Cabbie, and other Harm City legends. This male of the Homo Foodstamponid branch of our devolutionary tree, is—merely reprehensible!

Just after 6:00 this morning, Merely Reprehensible strolled in as Angie—who is retired, but can't make her gas & electric payment, so has to work the FFFFF register for the morning breakfast crowd stopping in for their bagels, doughnuts and yogurt on their way to work—logged onto her cash register.

He is a middle-aged white man who owns a small construction company and employs a mangy thirty-something drowned rat of a helper, who stood by nervously as they shopped and then cut into line with a full basket of meat and ice cream just ahead of a coffee and doughnut order. By the time his $218 worth of steaks and nutty buddy bars were rung up, there were three additional single item customers stuck in line behind him.

Then, as the order was totaled, and Angie said, "Enter your pin number Sir", the order was denied, as he had entered the wrong pin number. This was retried numerous times. We now had six customers in line. Angie then paged the manager, who paged the courtesy babe, who called Merely Reprehensible over to the window so that he could call up the junkie that had sold him an EBT card with $220 on it for $100 dollars.

We were now eight working stiffs deep at the register as our NFL representative [he was wearing

The Ghetto Grocer

Baltimore Ravens attire] kept questioning the junkie on the other end of the land line as to the correct pin number. We can only presume that the junkie knew his baby's mama's pin number. However, he had apparently injected sufficient liquid assets into his bioconomy to render him Simply Incomprehensible.

The man and his helper said they would be 'right back', and left the store. Angie rang out her customers, placed the nutty buddys in the freezer, rolled the meat into the meat room, and saved the receipt. By 8:00 she was swamped by legit customers. By 9:00, when I left, the nutty buddys were looking right lonely.

Okay, let's say next month, when Merely Reprehensible and his emaciated helper show up to commit food stamp fraud, the Zombie Apocalypse hits. What will my last act as an FFFFF clerk be before the Zekes overrun the store?

I will grab a 24 ounce longneck glass bottle of Everfresh mango-carrot flavored juice beverage, and use it to brain the emaciated helper. I will then kick his employer in the balls with my steel toe boot. Then, as I tell the FFFFF employees and customers to flee out the back door behind produce, I will deploy my trusty case cutter, eviscerate the helper, and use his entrails to tie his employer down on Angie's now pretty funky register—sorry Angie.

In this way, as we make our way out the back and leap off of the produce dock, we will know that the Zekes are coming as soon as Merely Reprehensible ceases his I'm-being-eaten-alive-and-this-is-not-cable-TV-and-therefore-really-sucks howls of anguish.

You know, I thought Jack Donovan was nuts when he evoked the 'zombie apocalypse' as a solution to liberal feminism. But you know what Jack: I think I'm stoked for this thing. There is more than enough zombie bait to go around in this town.

Disclaimer

No zombies were abused, injured or mistreated in the composition of this work.

'Junkie Juice in Aisle Nine': A Survey Of Subhuman Stains in Harm City Eateries and Food Markets

© 2014 James LaFond

"Please Lord don't let me die in a supermarket!"

-Miss Ezz

Last night I was breaking down three dairy pallets in the stockroom, when a local heroin dealer and a junkie walked through to the bathroom. This dealer uses the men's room at Free Food For Fat F...s to sell dope to people that need help firing up.

The dealer is a forty-year old black man who constantly mumbles cusswords. It is as if Richard Pryor was drunk, angry and stumbling around trying to memorize his jokes. I think this dude does this to project an air of menace and to keep people away. His junkie was an emaciated white boy of perhaps 20. They came through mumbling and cussing to no one in particular at 12:05.

Three employees attempted to access the two toilet men's room over the course of the next half hour. By 12:30 the dealer was gone, cussing furiously to himself as he walked by me. Finally Zach tried to use the urinal and came back out in disgust, asking me how long the junkie had been there. I responded, "He must be having a hard time. The guy that helped him fire up just left in disgust. With any luck the coroner will be carting him off under a sheet in a few hours."

Zach grabbed the night captain, who spent the next 10 minutes watching the bathroom drama. By the time I was out on the floor with my freight at 12:40 the junkie was staggering around the store. The night captain spent the next hour as the personal security guard and safety manager for the stoned junkie, who never ended up buying a thing.

Junkies in Winter

About 15 years ago a KFC I used to walk by was closed down after a body was found to have been in the men's room for 2 days.

The Ghetto Grocer

The same year I saw a junkie overdose in the men's room of a supermarket I worked in.

In December Scabby Abby was caught shooting heroin in the women's room at Wal-Mart.

Earlier this winter a junkie was found dead in a Burger King close to where I live, having been draining in the bathroom for an entire day.

Last Friday, at the local Dunkin Doughnuts a junkie overdosed in the men's room, and was revived by the cops and EMTs.

This past Sunday Miss Ezz, bookkeeper at Cheap Guys R Us in West Baltimore, called me.

"You would not believe what I've had to put up with this week with these ghetto cashiers and these drug dealer customers. We sell fifty cases of garlic powder a week [25 times normal]. The drug dealers put it in their coke and heroin to throw off the police dogs. Then, on Saturday night this junkie dies in the men's room, a needle sticking out of his arm. Nobody missed a beat. The EMTs came and tried to revive him. The cops came and taped off the area. The CSI people and the coroner come. They eventually wheel the body out, and we keep pumping out the groceries; customers pushing their shopping carts of sodas and oodles of noodles around the corpse on the gurney. Nobody even blinked. Please don't let me die in one of these places—please!

"Then I have to use the woman's room—a regular pit of filth; women pissing on the walls—how does someone without a dick piss on the wall? The generals [janitors] sign the bathroom log, but they just take a dirty mop and push the germs around. It is bad enough that I have to use this room, then I get inside and the light does not work. The first thing I think is I might be tripping over a body! I had to prop the door open with the trash can to let in enough light—someone should just condemn the neighborhood."

I would like to recommend needle exchange stations at the entrance to supermarket restrooms, a Pink Floyd music feed in the men's room, as well as crime tape and a body bag in the janitorial closet. Bleeding hearts feel free to improvise your own Junkie aid station. In the meantime bring on the China White.

Six-to-One: The Cop Thug Matrix

© 2014 James LaFond

Yesterday morning, at 8:33, 4/8/14, I was leaving Free Food For Fat F...s as a cop interviewed our boss and a cashier about two emaciated white dirt-bags who grabbed and got gone with some groceries.

It required one cop, for a half hour, just for the documentation. The creeps now need to be found and dealt with.

I walked down the road through the nice middleclass neighborhood where I typically see two motorists pulled over just before midnight by the cops from the overnight shift. I usually see two cruisers at the 7-11 this time of morning. They are absent, hopefully kicking the shit out of the dirt-bags.

At 8:54 I hit the parking lot of the Aldis box store to see customers lined up outside, and six cop cars parked around the sidewalk. An ambulance is pulling off with only one EMT driving. The sirens are not lit up and she takes her time. Is she the only one that responded, or is her partner in the back attending to someone?

I go over to the bus stop and observe. At 9:12 the cops emerge and the customers are allowed in. Two big muscular white cops are escorting a big muscular black dude who is limping, and has his hands cuffed in front of him. A towel is draped over his right arm. A backpack is brought out by another cop. All of the cops pull off. The cop that is hauling the innocent object of oppression pulls out five feet from me. I look down into the eyes of the man in custody, who is holding his right arm as if in great pain, and he looks up at me with eyes seemingly pleading for sympathy.

I didn't have any extra sympathy in my backpack so stood stone-faced. Granted these same cops pick on me simply for walking unafraid through this area at night. But I am glad for the Aldis staff that they have a strong presence here. They were on the scene for at least 40 minutes, and it could have been no longer than 70 minutes, as the store opens at 8:00. I hope that ambulance was empty, and no Aldis employee was being hauled off injured.

The Ghetto Grocer

These small box store operations sell food cheaply, largely because they are lightly staffed by low-paid female clerks, who never number more than 3 on the premises at one time. One girl is by herself at the register, one alone on the dock with the truck, and one straightening out the shelves center store. This morning's activity is typical for the food stamp rush you get from criminals. The cowardly whites will go into an operation with a lot of male employees, and in the confusion, grab something and run. The violent black criminals will either strong arm an isolated employee, or boldly begin hauling goods out, and then fight if stopped, demanding loudly that the merchandise belongs to them. I dealt with hundreds of both types as a manager and could not imagine the stress on some 100 pound middle-aged woman that would come from dealing with this guy that looked like LL Cooljay—dude, if I misused a consonant I apologize.

The larger view I took from this situation was the number of cops that were tied down by two scampering petty thieves and one strong-arm man. Last week it required 60 cops to detain two kids hunting legally with a beebee gun near my son's campus. What in the world is this Baltimore County precinct staff going to do—and they do seem to have quick response times, aggressive protocols, and efficient resolutions compared to the city cops—if let's say, 20 dope-fiends start grabbing and running and 10 big dudes start grabbing people? What about 200 fiends and 100 thugs?

I realize that cops largely pile on the way they do for safety and liability purposes, with three being normal for a traffic stop. But if this is the way they are used to operating, imagine what kind of stress these police will be under if, for some reason, the thugs and dopefiends do not get their EBT money one month and come out in force. Let's not even think about if the power grid goes down. When I ran a city supermarket I was usually outnumbered by criminals at any given time by about five-to-one. I stood up to them effectively because they knew I had a girl in the office behind plexiglass with a phone that would bring cops in five minutes. What if the cops are all busy up the street, and the thugs know it? What about three ladies alone in an unattached building? What if a significant slice of our criminals [hundreds in the area I walked through yesterday morning, and thousands in the similar-sized area where I live in the city] decide to grab and go? What if that day ever comes?

Crack Hos & Heroin Honeys: One Night in a Supermarket Restroom

© 2014 James LaFond

Last night, 4/11/14, I arrived at Free Food for Fat F...s at 11:27. As I approached the store front I noticed one bum sleeping on the sidewalk, one stoner twitching and rocking on the curb, and one crack head pacing before the front door, hassling the two customers ahead of me about something. As I entered the fool tried to block my progress and I shouldered by him and he said, "Sir? Sir?? Sir???"

After his pleas for whatever he wasn't going to get went unanswered three times he followed me a few steps and said, "I hate it when you people act all retarded. Can't you people hear what I'm saying?"

All of those fools were white, a demonstrable display of what Anglo-American culture has become in Drug War America.

I noticed, when I passed by the women's room to get to my refrigerated storage areas to begin processing the dairy order out in the stockroom, that the door to that facility did not close. Over the course of the next three hours I was back and forth through this hallway often. Something was the matter with the hinge. I had a large order, and a frozen order also, so did not take out time to jot down the times of the following occurrences. I can, however, give approximate times.

12:00 a.m.: A worn out old crack-ho—an emaciated bleach-blonde with cadaverous skin stretched over poorly formed bones—was smashing a rock of crack up on the women's room sink and snorting it. She would then cough up a wad of oral secretions, launch it onto the floor, and smash another rock, which she would then snort with all of the grace of my mother's old dust-buster. She walked past me with a mumbled 'goodnight' as she left through the stockroom.

12:30 a.m.: A fat white woman and a scrawny black dude went back into the women's room and smoked a hit of crack cocaine. They were all business, in and out in ten minutes.

The Ghetto Grocer

1:30 a.m.: Two soaking wet white trash hos of hoggish proportions, wearing spandex and heavy makeup, ho hoop earrings dangling from their pale beefy lobes, were escorted past me by a small black man of extremely dark complexion and smiling continence. He is a drug dealer who has used our facility before and he cheers up and says, "Hey Yo" as he herds his heifers on by. They all three repair to the two stall women's room. I do not know what transpired in the plush accommodations as I went up front for my coffee break. Fifteen minutes later, as I sat on the bench at the front door, they walked out through the register lane without making a purchase, laughing and giggling all the way. He flashed an ivory smile at me and escorted his portly harem out the door.

2:30 a.m.: Officer Manfriendly, my personal oppressor, walked in to use the men's room in his paramilitary getup. As I inventory his Batman utility belt it occurs to me that the women's room is definitely the place to fire dope and smoke crack.

3:00 a.m.: A very attractive couple enters and begins shopping with a basket. She is tall, elegant, and white, not busty enough to pose in playboy, and not thin enough to model clothes. She is beautiful in the very high heels she can barely stand on, doing the dopefiend lean as she is. Her date is a short muscular black man with his pants actually buckled around his waist. They are in their late twenties and he can't keep his hands off of her as she staggers and drools in the aisle. He has a powder blue hat. She carries a finely stitched black leather purse about the size of one of her shoes. They cannot decide who should be pushing the cart. They head back to the women's room and have sex standing up, between the stall doors and the sink, with the door wide open. She is bent over the sink and he is having a hard time getting his pelvis level with her rather remarkable Caucasian ass. She is spreading her legs to get lower for him. When I pass again coming back from the cooler he has had the decency to push her up against the wall so that she is not exposed to passersby. After their ten minute tryst they shop for another 20 minutes and then leave hand-in-hand.

3:30 a.m.: The frozen food man is walking in the front door. I am taking my lunch up on the bench waiting for him. We sort the frozen order together on Saturday mornings. He is being followed by a fifty year old crack head who asks him for a ride to his house no less than nine times, which is how many times I counted the question. In between each request for a lift Rob says the following, sometimes repeating his answer after the next repetition of the plea for a 'lift man':

"No man, no."

"I'm not losing my job to give you a lift dude."

"Hey asshole, how many ways do I have to say no?"

"Get lost you loser!"

"Ask him [the night captain] to call a cab for you."

"Get the fuck away from me man!"

"You're a sentence away from losing the rest of your teeth pal!"

I punched in with Rob as the night captain called a cab for the crack-head, who then disappeared into the night like a phantom, not wanting a cab at all. When we got back to the walk-in freezer around the corner from the restroom he went on a rant, "What a trashy neighborhood this is. I was in a good mood, now I'm all torqued up over that loser. What has happened to the white race? They're worse than the niggers!"

The Ghetto Grocer

I responded, "Then you'll be glad to know that they aren't reproducing. All the white dudes come in stoned or drunk, and alone. The white girls come in stoned or drunk with sober black dudes. According to the sexual activity in the women's room there the trash of the future is going to be brown."

He grabs the ice cream rack and looks at me in dismay, "Can you imagine how stupid that generation 'ill be!"

Spring is sprung and all is sloth out in the Narcostate.

The Ghetto Grocer, over and out.

Shinny Things: A Ghetto Grocer Heads Up

© 2014 James LaFond

You, American Consumer, hero of the resource depletion epic, wish to pursue your purpose with the purest food and in the cleanest environments. You wish to consume both quality and quantity, and to be untroubled by lack of plenty; desiring fresh vegetables in winter and fresh meat out of olfactory range from the slaughter yard. As you were raised with a raging sense of entitlement and now pursue your living in an economy that may have you up and toiling away at any hour of day or night, you also wish to have access to these things at low prices and 24/7. Any food retailer with the means, who is not buried deep in the ghetto, will seek to facilitate this need for New York/Vegas style around-the-clock consumption.

These concerns with fresh food, cleanliness and low prices intersect in one of my favorite places, the supermarket olive bar.

Due to your commercial conditioning, which plays on your simian attraction to shining things, you equate shinny with clean. As a master of the janitorial arts and long time retail food ubergeek, I feel it is my duty to explain to you what exactly that glaze on you kalamata olives consists of.

You wish the lowest prices. Therefore your retailer will strive to incur the lowest costs. For instance, the clean appearance of a retail food floor, indicated in your simian brain, by its shine, is of the utmost concern. One achieves this by quarterly stripping and waxing which is very heavy on noxious chemicals which literally dissolve the shoes and respiratory tissues of the floor strippers. The shine is then maintained by nightly buffing with a propane powered buffer that uses buffer pads that spin at a high velocity. This was formerly done with a low-speed electronic buffer, but that takes too long, requiring an 8 hour work night for the floor tech. To get the job done in 5.5 hours the high-speed buffer—which sounds like a Harley Davidson motorcycle revving inside a building and damages the hearing of all present—must be employed.

The Ghetto Grocer

The down side of the high-speed buffer is that it liquefies particulates and sprays them at high speed all about. I was once slashed by a loose razor that was cast thirty feet by a buffer and still had the velocity to cut through my jeans. The resulting liquefied wax that is sprayed on the lower shelving makes bottom shelves and refrigeration unit kick plates impossible to keep clean.

There is another problem though: the dirt tracked in on customer shoes, the meat particles tracked out of the butcher's room, and the urine and fecal matter tracked out of the restrooms, which are open to the public. How does one clean that?

1. sweep with push broom

2. edge with wet mop

3. sweep with whisk broom

4. scrub with floor scrubber [a really excellent cleaning device that utilizes liquid cleaner, water and suction tubes along with a sponge trap]

5. Sweep with push broom

6. Buff at the lowest speed possible

Due to the need to trim cost and hence hours steps 1,3 & 5 are almost always skipped, and the buffer is cranked up to maximum speed and run at a fast walk, maximizing filth projection from 3 inches to 4 feet off the ground.

Since the store is open 24 hours, open salad bars and olive bars and hot food displays are pasted with this unsavory glaze. Stores that are closed overnight are therefore preferable as these open food displays will be removed or covered— supposedly. Of course, if you are shopping discount or in a union-staffed store, hours will be cut to the bone and the olive bar will be left open overnight to receive this nasty patina.

The onerous job of floor tech has been passed down the economic latter over the past 30 years across the following ethnic groups, demonstrating the unhealthy nature of the occupation:

1980s white

Early 1990s blacks

Late 1990s Eastern Europeans

2000s Latin Americans

The Ghetto Grocer

I will never forget my history teacher laughing at how stupid a tribe of Indians was who sold Manhattan Island to the Dutch for some glass beads. Then I found out that they were selling some other tribe's island and changed my mind as to who the villains and dupes were.

In any case, it seems that people in Eastern North America have long been willing to trade a clean environment and untainted food for shinny things. The next time you are tempted to admire the shinny floor at your local retail food emporium, be mindful of the liquefied wax and filth that has been sprayed like a fine glaze upon everything from ankle to nipple. You might want to do more than rub that apple on your shirt before you bite into it.

Bon appetite!

WIC Reality: The Ghetto Grocer on the Malleability of Your Collective Will

© 2014 James LaFond

After reading my most recent Breeder's Digest [#21, Breeding, Feeding and Culling in Harm City] a male reader became incensed that food stamp recipients are using 'my tax dollars' to by $200 designer cakes and steamed shrimp. He went on to expound on his collective utopian point, "They should be made to buy basics: ground beef, chicken, vegetables. I work with this guy who makes the same as me, yet he lives with a woman who has five kids by five different guys, who pays almost nothing for rent. This guy gets to eat off of her food stamps and has no bills. It isn't fair. It's not what the

Founding Fathers meant to be. How can it be this way? I want these poor children fed, but the food isn't even going to them but to these deadbeat dads! There has got to be a better way to feed people."

I did what I could to comfort the fellow, "Welfare has no relation to feeding the hungry. It is about transferring wealth from one group to another in order to grow the government and foster the kind of antagonism you are feeling, which will grow the domestic military arm of the government exponentially when these sentiments are no longer contained by the belief in the fairy-tale Founding Fathers, who were just a bunch of scumbag slavers who wanted to cut the Home Country out of the profit scheme. Any empire requires a threatening parasite class to which funds are funneled away from the fearful productive class. The state provides the force matrix that feeds the parasite class and protects the productive class, making it equally indispensable to both sides, and assuring its growth in response to unrest from either segment of these two enslaved groups. Inequity is built in as the driving dynamic of the system and cannot be dispensed with."

He looked at me with bug eyes, "Say what? What does that mean?"

"It means you're locked in to a deliberately unfair system that has just begun to put the squeeze on you. As to your point about a nutrition-based system for feeding the poor, the closest thing we have is called the WIC program and it is administered by the Department of Agriculture. Vouchers are distributed one per month per child, in addition to a fruit and vegetable check for every WIC family. That is a six to ten dollar value. The standard check either provides formula for infants or surplus American grown foods. The fact that you believe that this corrupt system can be fixed, and that you can be counted on to vote for the corrupt politician who promises to fix it, fuels the system and grows the government that owns you."

He looked at me as if he were going to cry, and then thankfully a luxury car commercial came on the TV in between the 7th and 8th innings of the ballgame we were watching, causing his eyes to glaze over, and the impact of my unsettling words to fade. By the time that American Ninja Warrior began broadcasting he had no other concern but celebrity and consumption, thankfully putting to rest the demons I had let loose in his mind. In the future some lying politician will no doubt effect an inoculation against any future attempts to infect his mind.

In case you are interested what a WIC check for a child between 6 months and 5 years redeems for, I, your friendly neighborhood Ghetto Grocer, have provided a list below. The cost is of course variable as it is redeemed for retail. However, most items must be generic or store brand to qualify:

2 gallons of milk

1 dozen eggs

1 half gallon of unsweetened juice

36 ounces of unsweetened or moderately sweetened cereal

16 ounces of American cheese

16 ounces of whole wheat bread

16 ounces of dried or canned beans or 18 ounces of peanut butter

Mister Twix: Ten Minutes in the Life of A Writer

© 2014 James LaFond

Yesterday I went down to Fort Hoodrat to buy some aloe juice which they have on sale, and which I like because it reminds me of that time that I snuck into the refrigerator as a little brat and drank from the bowl of gelatin that Mom was letting set up.

The tenth of the month is peak food stamp time and this is a food stamp store. Non-express orders are two carts deep, and even though the mamas usually have about $500 on their card, they cannot do math and rely on the cashier to laboriously deduct items from orders that go over, which is most of them. What we call 're-shop' is at plague proportions during the food-stamp cycle. Clerks are actually schedule just to put back 'what mama couldn't add up'.

I had two choices, an express lane with one lady and five items, and the other express lane with about 15 items and two lunch orders behind her. I get in line behind the lady with five items.

Her first item rings up for '2 for $5' and she says, "Oh no, the sign said it only two-ninety-nine."

The clerk said, "Okay, I'll go check."

The second-generation Latino man behind me has bananas, a Gatorade and a six pack of Twix candy bars. He breaks open the pack and grabs a bar and starts eating impatiently.

Two minutes later the cashier comes back with the items and says, "The sign says two-ninety nine for one, two-for-five if you get two. They are two-for-five."

The woman was aghast, "Oh baby, that ain't right—you gonna up da price on me 'cause I buyin' two. Shoot, take them off the order."

The Ghetto Grocer

The man behind me nudges me and nods at the cashier, "Can you imagine doing that for a living?"

"I used to."

"You used to do that?"

"Worked in retail food for thirty-five years—my three months on the register was hell. This kid is just lucky he doesn't have to call his supervisor for a card swipe. This place is set up for this. In a chain store, we'd be waiting for the bookkeeper to get done selling a stack of lottery tickets so she could come out and authorize the void."

The two items are now voided and the total is $14 something. The lady swipes her EBT card and it turns out that $5.96 worth of her order is not 'foodstampable'. The Latino man breaks out another Twix bar and asks, "What is 'foodstampable'?"

"It must be edible and, if it is a service-prepared food—like a deli item, or steamed shrimp—it may not be bought hot, but must be sold out of the cold case."

He shakes his head as another customer gets in line behind us, the last three having gone over to the other lane. "Man, we should have gotten into that lane."

"Yeah, but it's six deep now. If we cut in front it's our ass."

He eyes the two four hundred-plus pound women in the express lane with their seventeen year old male children towering in tow, as Mamma leans on the ill-fated shopping cart. "I got you brother." This dude is like a buck-twenty.

Then, as the woman fails to find her cash bills down in her cavernous bra cup, where I suppose you'd need a team of Nigerian Special Forces Commandos to actually get in and out alive, she turns to us very sweetly, and says "I'm sorry sirs," pulls out a plastic zip-lock bag from her purse full of change, and dumps it on register belt!

The poor kid running the register regards the heap of pennies, nickels, dimes, quarters, and other coins and coin-like objects, with a thousand yard stare. Mister Twix eyes a gap in the other lane hopefully and the giant woman opposite glares at him and closes the gap. He then grabs another Twix bar and quips, "Shit, I'll be done lunch by the time I'm done here. You drink that aloe shit for some kind of health reason or something?"

"No, I like the taste."

"Are you kidding me! My papa drank that shit right out of the root, pulp and all. Give me a Pepsi!"

He then picks up a bottle and starts checking the settled contents at the bottom, "Oh hell no—man I'll live a short life before I drink this shit. What kind of work you do now since you got away from this," he said indicating the kid who was sorting the bus tokens and Canadian coins out from the American legal slender.

"I write."

"You write books—you wrote a book?"

"Yes, I write an article or two a day for my website and am always working on a book project."

"How many books have you written?"

"Thirty-one, but I've only had twenty-four published so far."

"What kind of books?"

"History, violence, boxing, horror, sci-fi—seven categories all together."

"You make a lot of money?"

The kid looks up from his pile of quarters—he has the right idea—so I say loud enough for him to hear in case he is an aspiring writer, "I make a few hundred dollars a year—over six-hundred last year."

"Mister Twix says, "Damn, that's all," as the cashier mouths 'Fuck that,' and goes to counting out a stack of dimes, while the customer is helpfully sorting the change into denominations.

"No best sellers?" says Mister Twix as he grabs another candy bar and starts to munch.

"Well, my best seller sold about 3,000 copies I think over about 10 years. When it came out, this millionaire knife maker—it was a book on getting stabbed—asked for a free copy from the publisher, and then wrote an article based on it, for which he got paid two-hundred and fifty bucks, which was about the size of my first royalty check. Ten years later, when it goes out of print some Japanese guy who has held on to ten mint copies sells them for two-hundred-and-fifty a piece. Hell I only got ninety-four cents a piece!"

The kid is now discussing a large coin with the lady who insists it is a silver dollar. He has to take it to another cashier to confirm.

Mister Twix is enjoying our conversation, "Fucking Japanese business man homes, what do you expect?"

"I'm no business man, just a writer. I do have an agent though and he's sayin' my stuff would sell better as comics."

The young dude is back, having confirmed the coin is a half dollar, and gives me a look like, 'Hello pops, nobody reads books any more—of course comics will sell better.'

The coins, now stacked by denomination like a rugrat's play pirate treasure, the count proper begins. Mister Twix nudges me, "So what about this stabbing book—what the fuck?"

"I interviewed dudes who got stabbed—in prison, by their wife, in fights. I interviewed dudes who stabbed people. I interviewed witnesses. There was this one really badass knife fight between a guy in a

Latino gang in Chicago and this guy from an Italian gang, witnessed by the younger brother of the Latino dude."

Mister Twix says, "The Latino dude won, of course!"

"Yeah, the Italian guy went down with a perforated liver and punctured lung."

Now on his fifth Twix bar my new friend says, "That's what I'm talkin' about. Make that shit a comic!"

Finally, with a sigh of relief, the woman collects her unspent pennies and her groceries, and is off. I am checked out in a matter of seconds and turn to shake hands with my new friend, who says, "Nice meeting you man—go write some books."

'Another Chance for Men': Bridget Calls For Harm City Masculinity

© 2014 James LaFond

Out in Harm County, on Officer Manfriendly's beat, at Free Food For Fat F…s, where I toil for Boss John, whose ditch is ever in need of being filled with dirt, or of having said dirt removed, I work closely with about a dozen fellows, and not-so-closely with about a dozen others. The balance of the staff consists of perhaps 80 women.

Of these 24-odd men only two would be worth a sweat in a fight: Steevo of 'Running From The Cops' fame, and Bob, the big angry Polish-American who I help with the frozen food in the wee hours. This morning Bob told me a tale that warmed my combative heart.

"Yesterday Fruit Cake [our mild-mannered supervisor] gathered us up: me, that bagger twerp;

the worthless kid over in produce; and Sissy Boy
from the meat room, and told us we needed to walk
this woman home. She was definitely afraid, and
was not one of your typical toothless locals—in her
twenties. We never saw the guy, but she said he
followed her to the store, and that he had raped her
before. She only lived around the corner. Imagine
my confidence walking with a twerp, a twit, a sissy,
and a tinker bell off down the alley. I have to admit,
smacking some dirt bag's face into the pavement on
company time did have me looking on the positive
side.

"We never saw the guy, but this girl was terrified.
As soon as we got within ten doors of her house she
broke into a run—ran for her life with her little
grocery bag dangling, and there is Sissy Boy—
basketball tall—trying to hunch down and hide
behind us! Could you imagine being such a gutless
turd, getting up in the morning and having to look
at that in the mirror? Of course, he is such a sweetie
pie he was probably afraid he would get raped!
Dude, get it over with and jump from the Key
Bridge!"

In my mind, this was a huge deal. Just as the city has
been overrun by violence on the eve of summer so
has the county. The fact that women are now asking

for male protection, and that a business would permit its employees—in this legalistic age—to escort a customer home, does provide a ray of hope.

When I worked in the city as a store manager my legally shell-shocked employer did not even want me escorting little old ladies to and from their car for fear I or the criminals that preyed on them would get hurt and then file a law suit. I still guaranteed the protection of my customers and coworkers on the property to the best of my ability. This remained a bone of contention between myself and my employer until I tossed the keys to my co-manager one Tuesday morning and made an exodus from my own little Egypt.

The fact that four of the five men in the above case were in no way psychologically prepared for any type of confrontation, yet went out of their way to protect this lady despite their fears, makes their actions all the more commendable. [Bob had sadistic ulterior motives.] This type of protective manly behavior was once commonplace in America, but is now largely absent. I hope that one of the side effects of our deteriorating economy, which lies prostrate at the feet of the rising narcostate, is an increase in this kind of spontaneous community policing.

Bubba and the Mud Sharks: Cautionary Supermarket Pickup Tales from the Ghetto Grocer

© 2014 James LaFond

I used to work in an all night Harm City supermarket with Israel and The Mac Daddy, two big bruthas who, with studied unaffection, referred to each other as 'Silvaback' and 'Big Boy'.

Silvaback was old school and up from Georgia, and preferred 'big-boned womenz with a good bit a thigh'. He maintained a stable of honeys forty years his junior as he was a prosperous slumlord, and worked a good-paying fulltime job. Permit me to give you an idea of his taste in women...

We were breaking down a pallet of juice and noticed that we were both looking at Liz, bending over in front of us, working register lane candy from a tote box. This surprised me as he had repeatedly decried the bony nature of 'white girlz' and gave The Mac Daddy, who had a taste for the pale ladies, a hard way to go for not 'stayin' wit 'is own'. But I suppose there is an exception to every rule under heaven. I decided to bust him for crossing the line, at least in his mind. "So you like that man?"

Keep in mind, that while naturally blonde, of sweet disposition, and very pretty, Liz had a **huge** butt that you could set a beer can on. She hated her butt, and did everything she could to hide it, and would no doubt have been horrified that we had caught this wide angle view quite by chance. Silvaback stood straight, grinned wide, and said, "Yeah, I likes me that fine lille butt!"

I was in shock. As a nominally white man who likes big butts, I thought I was extreme. But as wide as Ray Lewis' shoulders is not 'lille' by any scale I'm versed in.

Now The Mac Daddy, of the hip hop generation, liked fit white women. Always cognizant of potential sexual harassment charges I did everything I could to avoid working with him while the upscale SOBO babes were doing their after nightclub shopping. But The Mac Daddy followed me like a hound, as he noticed that my 'real white boy' longhaired temporary appeal to upscale women who were drunk and pissed off at the lawyer they had shacked up with, might possibly generate 'a lonely friend of her's' for him to 'pickoff'.

I might be in the aisle explaining the difference between young tender peas and Grade A Fancy peas to some six-figure bitch-on-wheels who was really interested in me disrespecting her for an hour a week while her old man raided a mutual fund, and he would come up to me, put his hand on my shoulder like he was my gay pimp, and say something like, "Jim here my white Mandingo Baby. Cain't go wrong with my man—you got a sista Baby?" Or he might declare that we were "tag-team partners in the art of luv", "ebony en ivory fo variety" etc. I could not count how many times I literally ran from this guy while in the presence of one of these high-strutting snob-babes.

This type of thing was really humiliating. I had three different regular customers, all single feminist home owners, come up to me in the aisle when I was alone with a check list and pen, interviewing me for their open houseboy or boy toy slot. I suppose this is done online now. I was 35 and these chicks were 45. The entire aspect of bussed in manual laborers [male and female, Liz had at least 30 suitors] being selected and pursued as sex workers for the local rich was unappealing to my militantly antisocial mindset. The Mac Daddy worked it though, milked it for what it was worth. Silvaback, he did not concur. He could not understand why "Some Big Boy would want ta layup with some lady who back might break, unda 'is dumb black ass—den he up for assault!"

I actually had to employ a local stay-behind white trash wench to scare off one of these prissy suitors. On another occasion I had a criminal friend talk another stalker out of following me around town after I got off work

There was one drunk lady, a tall fifty-year-old tanned blonde, who must have been quite a beauty in her youth, who actually put her hand on my chest one July 4th and French kissed me in front of the Green's ice cream case. She then asked me if we had any vanilla ice cream without the vanilla specks because it was going to be licked off of her body by her husband. I got her the ice cream while she leaned on me and purred. Then she told me that her husband and her had sailed their yacht up from Florida and asked if I would clock out and come down to the pier with her, that they would pay me double what I would make on the night. I declined—in my mind imagining her husband's Bosnian Merc bodyguards dumping my snuffed body out at sea—and she gave me another kiss and left. A female coworker saw this, and then when she questioned me and I told her, she tore off her apron and ran for the front door, "Why'd you let her go asshole. For four hundred I'll do her and her old man!"

Now, at 2 to 3 in the morning it got to be fun when the upscale strippers would come in to shop with their bodyguards. These were girls we could identify with who had no agenda where we were concerned.

It was not only heterosexual advances that were targeted at us overnight clerks. There was this tall hairy auto-mechanic who worked in overalls at the local garage by day, and came in by night wearing a wig, an open blouse to reveal his masculine chest, and a woman's tube top as a skirt with no underwear. I once had two gay guys ask me if we had any Edy's mint chocolate chip ice cream in the case. I knew there was some there. But the case was messed up. I kept digging until I found it. When I turned—still on my knees as someone had buried the last of this flavor in the back of the bottom shelf—I looked up behind me to see three flaming gay guys admiring my backside and grinning like Freddie Mercury's clones.

Such are the humiliations heaped upon the youthful store clerk. Now, past mating age, I turn such situations into excuses for humor. Recently, a young lady came up to me while I was stocking the yogurt section—quite expertly I might add—and asked me, "Sir, do you work here?"

I turned, sporting my newly grown white beard, and said with the utmost gravity, "Miss, I don't normally work in supermarkets, but when I do, I work at Mister John's Food Mart."

So, last Friday night, as I broke down freight in the stockroom, I was interrupted by two drunk women in their late teens, both about six feet tall, one about 200 pounds and cute in shorts and a loose blouse. The other was about 140 pounds, very pretty, and dressed like a rap video dancer. This woman and her bodyguard were obviously looking for companionship that was old enough to buy them more alcohol. The hot one approached me—in this dark dingy stockroom with a blackened-from-filth concrete floor—with that 'I know you like what you see and I'm going to use it against you until I milk you to a grayed husk and cast you aside for a fresh meal ticket' gleam in her baby blue eyes. I rudely ignored this slut as I loaded U-Boats of freight. They went away.

They came back in a couple times that night, making their rounds, trying to determine which of the passably fit guys they could make their mark on before they sobered up disastrously. At 2:30, terribly close to sober, and not willing to have sex for booze behind the dumpster with the homeless guys out back, but looking for someone to take back to their apartment who they could stomach having breakfast with, the two ladies, the wallet-crusher and her support element, homed in like sorrow-seeking drones on Bubba.

I was seated reading on my break ten feet from where Bubba operates the register. Bubba is almost seven feet tall and these very tall ladies truly liked him, unlike the callous offer 'to use and be used' earlier directed at me. Bubba is 19 and is a virgin, which is shocking in this day and age. If I was single and south of forty, I would have been hooking up with these girls. At Bubba's age I would have been silly putty in their manicured hands.

The Ghetto Grocer

They actually bought something they did not need to talk to him, tried to have a real conversation, and even asked for his phone number. He blew them off and they walked off, waiving and winking at me. I said, "Hey Bubba, at your age I would have given them my number. What don't you like about them? The big girl has a decent personality, and the slut is gorgeous. If you put them both together you could have a decent date."

He said, "I'm not interested. They're just mud sharks."

"What? What is a mud shark?"

"Look at them; one is fat, and the other one dresses like a whore. They obviously go for black guys— mud sharks!"

I laughed for hours. For an amateur anthropologist like me, the finding of a new term, particularly one that is a joint gender/race slur, was quite a find.

The Real Mothership: Conveyance Shoplifting and Ham Slice Ebo in The Hood

© 2014 James LaFond

I have some Black Muslim friends who are still waiting for the Mother Ship to dock above the pyramids and liberate them from their toilsome lot under the thumb of the feral white devils bred by Big-Headed Yakub on the island of Patmos some 5,700 years ago. However, in the meantime, one might choose to observe a more closely orbiting, but not so heavenly, body…

Shoplifting is an art, and when such a fool as Ham Slice Ebo screws it up to the extent that he did last Friday night, the Ghetto Grocer can only shake his head. Sure, shoplifters are the Ghetto Grocer's foes. But it is foes that make the hero. How is a ghetto grocer to learn the finer points of foiling shoplifters when a fool like Ham Slice Ebo shows blatant disregard for shoplifting procedures and etiquette?

Last Saturday morning at 2:30, Ham Slice Ebo, at five feet tall and 170, wearing a white T and beige cargo shorts with white socks and sneakers, walks into Free Food For Fat F...s, with his black Obama flip phone to his ear, ranting and raving about ham slices with whoever is using him for a shopping drone on the other end.

This person directs Ebo by memory, across the store, up and down aisles—"No, da uda way Yo"—until finally, after many dozens of uses of the F-word and N-word, Ebo stands before the ham slice display at the end of the aisle where I work Mister John's yogurt, in hopes that one chick who looks as if she eats yogurt instead of biscuits for breakfast actually walks in to buy some.

For five minutes Ebo debates Ham Slice pricing, weight, packaging, and possible side dishes such as 'Yeay, dat good tastin' shit' with The Voice of the Midnight Shopping Oz.

Finally, on the verge actually selecting a ham slice, Ebo shouts into the phone, "Oh I need ta ged me some hot pockets Yo."

The Ghetto Grocer

Midnight Shopping Oz—now on speaker—objects vociferously, but our hero forges on to frozen food. He soon returns with two boxes of breakfast pockets, wanders around in front of the ham slice case, and then asks me, "Where da batroom at Yo?"

I point out the 'batroom' and he ducks into the stockroom with his hot pockets.

Ebo enters the bathroom where Trent is using the urinal, takes the hot pockets into the stall, makes some tearing noises, and exits the stall.

Our villain, Trent, sly scheming snitch that he is, takes the boxes up front to Zach while Ebo returns to the ham slice case—pockets bulging—and continues his ham slice debate with Midnight Shopping Oz, still on speaker.

I head up front to buy a drink. As I am checking out and returning to Mister John's yogurt case, Ebo passes me, still discussing ham slices with his remote master. Zack confronts him with the boxes and says, "Empty your pockets and pay for these hot pockets and you can go."

This is where smart shoplifters break open their wallet and give you some bullshit story about being allergic to frozen food packaging, pay up, and get the hell out of Dodge. Not Ebo. "Oh, I ain't got no hot pockets!"

Ebo then returns to the ham slice case, resumes his conversation, and peruses the hams, looking for an opportunity to dump the hot pockets. Trent, however, snitch for The Man [whose real name is Mister John], continues his ham slice discussion with Oz.

Five minutes later, Oz and Ebo are still discussing ham slices as Trent tries not to fall asleep standing behind him, and I cut in the new tangerine Greek yogurt, which will hopefully bring the Ravens' Cheerleaders flocking to my workstation...

Did I mention that a squad of cops were stationed on the lot guarding against a gang of rampaging hoodlums, and that Ebo walked past them coming into the store?

Finally, a towering, middle-aged, redneck cop arrives, heel of hand on his Batman utility belt. He stands next to Ebo and says, "What's up?" which Ebo's multi-lingual device hanging from the chain around his neck—what else could it be?—should have translated as, 'Please run so I can slam your stubby ass to the floor.'

Ebo ignores the cop.

The cop repeats himself.

Ebo talks to Oz some more.

Another, younger, cop arrives.

He talks to Ebo.

Ebo mills around looking for his mouse hole and cannot find it.

The cop tells him to hand the phone over and he does. Oz has grown silent. He then searches Ebo and finds various things, among them hot pockets. His cargo shorts no longer look like special operations fatigues with blowout patches and spare ammo clips jammed in them.

Finally, hanging his head in childlike dismay, not understanding how his master plan unraveled, Ebo was taken away. Wherever Ebo was taken to, he will surly occupy the bottom notch on the food chain.

Yes, Ebo may seem pathetic. However, I have witnessed the proper handling of his type as an auxiliary shoplifter before. Perhaps Oz was training him, directing him on a remote dry run. You see, if Ebo had no outstanding warrants, and his hot pockets were worth less than $300 retail, he will be let go with a citation. Apparently he had a warrant, as the cops took him away.

That morning, on my way to training, Miss Ezz, one of my West Side connections, called me with a mother ship report. You see, a mother ship in shoplifting is a person in a wheel chair, or powered handicapped conveyance. They are only effective when they have runners like Ebo working with them. [You war gaming nerds recall how important it is to have infantry accompanying your panzers into Stalingrad...] But when they are effective, they strike it rich. If Ebo had been properly utilized by pairing him with a mother ship, the pilot of said blockade runner would have been able to make her escape as Ebo was occupying security with his boisterous incompetence.

Miss Ezz, take it:

"You would not believe the ghetto shit I'm looking at right now. Mind you, we have a security guard, a city cop—uniformed—and an LP detective on the premises. They're ready because food stamps just dried up. They're trying to haul this fat bitch up into the paddy wagon now. She's missing part of one leg and is in a wheel chair. They just caught her cruising out the door with over three-hundred dollars worth of Tide, bar soap, body wash—all stuff for resale.

"Can you believe this shit? I suppose after they chop the other foot off from her food stamp-induced diabetes she'll be able to haul more shit out of here. Don't get me wrong. I like my job. But sometimes, you think to yourself, 'Just drop a bomb already!'"

'Drug-head Dykes': And 'Mudshark Grannies': A Snapshot of the Ascendant Slave Mistress Class

© 2014 James LaFond

Just after midnight this morning I was breaking down my perishable freight in the stockroom as the dry grocery crew took their break up front. I start later as we share the same space and equipment in this congested old store. Night crews typically take their break after the freight is decked out on the floor. In a 24-hour store, instead of using the lunchroom, they will usually break up front so that the cashier is not alone and any customers can ask for help.

The Ghetto Grocer

Brown Fem Barbie

Ron and the boys were up front with Bubba when two 'drug-head dykes' came in. These two ladies of color were high on crack and were sucking face and grabbing ass in the aisle. Steevo did not mind one bit. The Ghetto Grocer was on the scene with an interview moments later and Steevo was still licking his lips:

"Yeah the fem had half her tatted-up ass hanging out, not saggy from the Tasty Cakes yet. I was liking that. Her dyke looked like a moldy muffin. Nevertheless I enjoyed the show until she went off. This stupid food stamp bitch started yelling at us for having freight on the floor, kicking the boxes, giving Ron shit. We should have slapped her. But the customer is always right, so we just sat there. But you know, a dumb bitch like that—that's just a cum dumpster anyhow—how can you not laugh at that?

"So maybe there's a smile. Then its on—fucking Ron up like she's his wife. He remained very polite and told her to call in the morning. He had to give her his name three times before she could remember it. 'Ron,' how fucking hard is that? That bitch had five hundred left on her EBT card after she bought her shit. I can afford but two-hundred a month for me and the wife and kid. All this bitch has got to do is drop babies and she's rolling in dough."

I then digressed. "Remember when you asked me what it would have been like to be a slave hundreds of years ago?"

"Yeah."

Well, according to the slave narratives it was often the slave mistresses—the wives of the masters—that were cruelest. Slave owners were essentially the same as welfare whores: they did not work, they drank where welfare whores get high, and they were very violent, just like ghetto bitches. Now, imagine that bitch owned you? Granted she owns you indirectly with the government acting as her proxy. Imagine that?"

"Oh I would kill that bitch in a heartbeat—even now—if she laid a hand on me."

"It wouldn't be her hand man. She'd have a gang of bouncers with whips and clubs and dogs to keep you in line."

"You mean like pigs fuck with us now?"

Steevo's anarchist education is coming along nicely.

Grand Mamma Mudshark

An hour later a 62-year-old woman, dressed like Daisy Duke, covered in faded tattoos, and so fat she has to ride a handicapped cart, came in shopping with her 16-year-old son. I thought to myself, 'Whoever knocked her up to keep her in food stamps until retirement was a better man than me.'

By the merchandise in their cart and the time of month I knew she was a foodstamper immediately. Everything that appeals to the compulsive welfare mentality has a greater margin built in. If food stamps were cut grocers would be laying off as much as 20% of their staff. People that shop with food stamps do not add—or perhaps can't. They let the register do it and leave the overage for the cashier to cart back to the shelf.

Now I was about to be shocked. What I thought was an unrelated customer was a 45-year-old half-sister to the mulatto son, who had a newborn baby in her second grocery cart! This was at 1:15 am. At 45-years-old this woman is still popping out babies to remain on the dole just like her mudshark mommy.

These ladies represent the aspirations of the majority of females in our growing underclass.

The Ghetto Grocer Op-Ed

What is most fascinating about this is that these female parasites actually constitute a leisure class. There is very little difference, in terms of incivility, violent propensities, and lack of self sufficiency, between the postmodern welfare queen and the English wives of the colonial plantation owners. The only real difference is that our modern slave-mistresses are not married to some dude who we might drag from his bed and burn, but to the U.S. Government.

Big Roy and the Boy: A Harm City Dialogue with Miss JoJo

© 2014 James LaFond

I interviewed Miss JoJo at the courtesy window of the ghetto supermarket where she is employed, asking her casually about her food stamp cycle two full days after the EBT rush reached its crescendo on Wednesday the 16th.

"It was pretty much your usual, threw out my back lifting hundreds of forty-two pound boxes of chicken wings at the register. A lot of your normal EBT bullshit with the customer putting two-hundred dollars more on the belt than they have on their card. Most of the people are pretty nice. We did have this one ghetto bitch with her gangbanger boy friend who was a dollar twenty-nine short. She looks at her old man and says, 'I need two dolla.'

"He just looks at her, and she keeps asking rudely. Eventually she says 'please' and he pulls out this knot-roll of money as thick as your fist and peels off two ones; five-hundred and forty dollars of my tax money so that this drug dealer with ten grand in his pants can eat steak and shrimp. It's kind of sad that so few EBT people can add, not even up to five dollars. The women are the dumbest by a long shot and they're generally callin' the shots because they have the card. I guess if you get pregnant when you're twelve that's pretty much it.

"The only ones that really get to me are the giant fat sweaty mammas who lay on their cart, sweat running down their face in sheets. This one bitch, when it came time for her to pay the taxable balance, reaches into her shirt, under her bra, underneath her sweaty watermelon titties, and pulls out this flattened wad of folded bills that is literally dripping with sweat. She flicks her hand so that the sweat sprays across the belt and then hands that shit over and I'm supposed to count it! Their breasts are like the community bank. As soon as they grow tits their shoving money and everything else down there.

"Last Sunday, just after noon ,this boy came in scared to death. He is a regular, lives five houses down the street with his mother and little brother. They are eight or nine. We never see her. The boys come in and buy milk and bread during the week. Well he was terrified, 'Miss JoJo you got to help me! This man is chasing me with a stick!'

"I took him into the booth with me and called his house—no answer of course. Mamma's not home. I took him out to Big Roy [the security guard] and now it was black on black so I just stepped back. Roy scowls down at him and points his big finger and says, 'Boy, you better not be lyin' ta me!'

"The poor kid breaks into tears, 'No, I wouldn't be lyin' ta you, no sir!'

"Then Roy gets the description and it's this dirt bag black panhandler, one of the crazies that run the street and gives everybody shit. The kid accidentally bumped into him and he went off trying to beat him with a stick. Big Roy walked him home and told me he knew the guy, that he was a low life, and that he's going to whoop his ass for going after the kid.

"It's so sad. These kids shouldn't have to raise themselves. They should get some time as children before the world shits all over them."

'Cutting Out The Man': Urban Hacks and Guerilla Courtesy

© 2014 James LaFond

The ghetto grocer does not usually shop in supermarkets—and that ought to tell you something about supermarkets. The conversation everywhere I go is about the increased costs of goods and services and the lack of increase in or the actual reduction in wages.

Retail food operators, being at the ass-end of the economy, have been trying desperately not to pass on increased costs to their customers for fear of having their customer base flee to a higher volume discount buyer such as Wal-Mart. So, to remain competitive, they have slashed wages and benefits, with the results that their own employees have become Wal-Mart's customers; the only place they can shop where the staff makes less than they do.

The Ghetto Grocer

Yesterday, as I left the market with my bottle of aloe juice, I ran into Miss Elsie, an older lady who was struggling with her bags. Miss Elsie lives near the store, a mere five-minute walk for me, ten minutes for her. I've carried her groceries home for her before and offered to do so again—hell, when she gets there she has two flights of stairs to ascend up the outside of the house to her third-story apartment. It must take her a half hour to ferry her bags up those stairs one at a time.

We stopped outside and she said, "I would call a cab but they take 15 minutes, and they are all foreigners and follow that GPS which takes them the wrong way sometimes and that costs. But mostly, I don't want to wait, because I have frozen foods and they don't always show up."

Melvin, the parcel pick up clerk, nodded to an older black man in a ball cap sitting on the bench, who has taken over Mister Jesse's hacking business since Mister Jesse got car-jacked, and said, "He's a good man."

The man tipped his hat to her as I eyed him up, something he took note of with a visible touch of discomfort.

Miss Elsie said, "How much?"

The hacker asked, "Where to?"

Miss Elsie answered, and then he said, "Five dollars."

He then led us over to his nice 2012 economy car, a two-door, with a large trunk which he had clear for groceries. A few minutes later Mister Gerald, the hacker pulled over in front of Miss Elsie's place and she gave him six dollars, "There you go baby. It usually costs me six and I have to wait, and tip the guy if I don't want the dirty look, and you are American."

I then quizzed Mister Gerald as to where he lived, where he worked, when he was available to drive, and otherwise vetted him for Miss Elsie. It turns out that he works second shift at a factory that has been cutting back and this is how he plans on paying for his car, by driving during the day for supermarket customers and not operating in the evenings like Mister Jesse did. Neither he nor Miss Elsie had a pen or paper, but I did. I took down his information and gave it to her as they discussed her weekly schedule. Mister Gerald mentioned that he would get cards made up soon. He had been hacking at the

Stop, Shop and Save stores that just closed. I verified this by dropping some management names and it turned out he knew them. Those stores have closed. Maybe Wal-Mart is coming to Harm City.

As I carried Miss Elsie's groceries up her 32 stairs she was feeling like she had hit the secure post-feministic lone nesting lottery, "You know Mister Gerald is such a nice gentleman. Thank you so much. I'll tell you what, when that goddamned African drove me to work the other day I about had a heart attack. He was doing fifty-sixty down side-streets at five a.m. in the dark!"

She then looked up at me with some concern and disparaged my appearance, "You know, for a guy who looks like he runs a racist gang, you are quite a gentleman yourself. It's a shame though, that beard puts fifteen years on you."

Off into the ghetto I went, looking to have a beer with a night-skinned babe in some hole-in-the-wall bar, quite pleased that Miss Elsie, self-described former 'wild-child of the sixties' disapproved of my beard of ethno-might, and also, that a baby boomer chick who once bought into all of the rampant feminist 'trust the government before you trust a man' bullshit decided to trust two men she knew with selecting an unlicensed driver for her, instead of trusting to the government's licensed African drivers.

Where I live most licensed businesses that are closely overseen by the State and Municipal authorities, such as liquor stores and cab and sedan services, have been taken over and staffed by Middle Easterners, Africans, Indians, and Eastern Europeans. Their prices are generally higher than the indigenous concerns they replaced. My policy now, is to spend my money at and recommend the unlicensed American businesses that have been springing up to serve the people who do not want to pay the additional 10-30% that the government licensed foreign businesses charge [which in all fairness just represents them passing on the cost of State fees, with their start-up licensing fees actually representing an infusion of foreign money into our centralized communist economy].

People like Mister Gerald and Mister Jesse [who got wiped out by a combination of criminal carjackers and the Baltimore City Police Department] and their impoverished customers like Miss Elsie [who does janitorial work in the mornings], represent a guerilla economy which is bound to be a growing concern.

Support your local gypsy cabbie, and look to your friends and neighbors for security rather than to the police, and you will be doing a small part in thwarting the cancerous growth of the global bazaar that is coming into full bloom under the Capitalist Caliphate.

The reader might note that most of the participants in this guerilla economy, who I have encountered, are over fifty, many over sixty.

Harm City Hit & Run: Just Trying to Get a Beer in Baltimore

© 2014 James LaFond

5:15 p.m.

An hour ago I headed down to the liquor store—the Korean one, not the Punjabi one, thank you very much. John, the owner, extended me the common courtesy of rounding down the taxes on the cheapest six-pack in his cooler. As I bore my questionable brew home Big Rich called me from East Baltimore, about his time in West Baltimore on the day crew at Stop, Shop & Run.

I stopped in at the hipster bar for one beer as Big Rich regaled me with the tale of...

Tide Yo!

A fine young man, his pants hanging below his knees just so, his hat cocked just so, seemed to have lost his way. The police officer on duty at this fine urban foods emporium noticed that the man had mistaken the front door for the register lane and walked over to render aid, customer service on his mind. The customer frantically kept trying to haul his two, two-gallon jugs of tide laundry detergent out of the cart, and kept being dragged back in, 'barely a buck-ten his self'.

Miraculously our hero yanked the [$50 retail, $20 resale] haul out of the cart, and made off, the cop hot on his heels, reaching for his tazer. Our hero made it to the head of the parking lot as the cop drew a bead on him. The stairs down to the parkway were concrete, and the cop did not want a dead shoplifter on his hands. He yelled for the customer to drop the jugs and he could go. He did so. Officer Thrifty brought the haul back to the store and then alerted cops and security stationed at nearby stores.

Within an hour, our hero, Tide Yo, fell for the bait and was collared by security at Bull's Eye Big Buys and hauled off to Central Booking.

One of the new White Vice Lords—tattooed teardrops and all—came into the bar selling women's deodorant and body wash he had just stolen from the drug store two blocks away. The going price was two dollars per unit. He seemed to be fully inked except for portions of his face.

Good Evening Sir

5:40 p.m.

I walked through the grassy courtyard of the church and the rectory where four young men smoked pot and drank malt liquor. The eldest said, "Good evening Sir" and I returned the courtesy.

As I came to the main drag a group of four younger teens were joking on my side of the street so I crossed. As I did so a 'thunk' 'clunk' 'ping' and 'moan' of metal and fiber glass sounded behind me.

A youth behind the wheel of an SUV with tinted windows had side-swiped a mail truck—one of those that look like a converted German WWII staff car—on the driver's side and dragged it out into the middle of the road. The four boys were cheering him on as he struggled to get it in gear.

I was now halfway cross a side street as he tore loose a piece of fiberglass fender from his driver's side, put it in reverse, whipped it around, and gunned it up the street. He then got stuck in traffic behind the cars at the next light and his engine died. He turned it over a few times, shifted, pulled his moaning door tight, and then got it started. He banked right so I leaped onto the sidewalk in time to avoid becoming the punch line.

He did about fifty going up the side street as the sounds of sirens began to converge from two fire stations. I saw an ambulance, a pumper, and a hook and ladder. The mail truck was not moving. The police chopper was headed out to the West Side.

Hopefully the postal employee is okay.

Aunt Jemima versus Hungry Jack: A Stovetop Race War!

© 2014 James LaFond

On Friday night as I stocked Mister John's yogurt at Free Foods For Fat F...s, I looked to my right, to the lady I have loved since I was twelve years old, the Land-o-Lakes Butter Babe, un-aged and immortal, still smiling at me while she kneels to her Whiteman and spreads out the cornucopia of plenty before spread...

...or so did my mind wander in my youth. Now though, as a crackpot intellectual barbarian, I worry about her extinction. As I sit in my plantation house in Sodom, just down the road in Gomorrah the owner of the Washington Red Skins is facing extinction if he does not change the name of his team. The federal government is putting him in its sights. Can my Lady Love be far beyond?

The Ghetto Grocer

Before I conclude my prediction and arrange for the defense of her sexist cult, permit me a digression to a simpler time, which has passed, as all three of the symbols of this particular high-carb race war have been disfigured or erased.

In the mid-1980s I worked the cereal section in a city market in the mornings, the last section to get freighted on Saturday morning as the shoppers came through the door. Since 1981 I had always been intrigued by the two following facts:

1. White shoppers always bought Aunt Jemima pancake mix, with the scarf-headed old auntie seemingly peering through time from the Antebellum South gracing the box with her unsightly and not yet picked or braided locks hidden, as many black women still do in the morning—I know, I've woken up with a few— prepared to fire up the griddle for her family.

2. Black shoppers always bought Hungry Jack pancake mix. It was a larger box, came in only three varieties to Aunt Jemima's five, and featured a big white man in overalls and a flannel shirt with hands on hips.

The Ghetto Grocer

This intrigued me. I wondered if perhaps customers, black and white, simply fell prey to the idea of a person from an antagonistic ethnic group serving them breakfast?

One Sunday morning at about 9 a.m. the answer came down my aisle. The following has formed into my brain as one of those treasured human experiences from my youth, that replays in my mind's eye every time I eat pancakes or stock that section in the store, indeed, even when I stock the Aunt Jemima frozen waffles and pancakes.

A black man and wife came into the aisle. The woman had one of those plastic clickers that my mother used to use to tally her purchases as she shopped. I suppose these folks would be in their late 60s about now. The man bent to grab the Hungry Jack pancake mix and the woman said, "Oh no you don't!"

The man looked up, hand still on box. "What?"

Woman: "What some big dumb Jethro-loookin' white muthafuca know about cookin' cakes!?!"

Hands were now on hips and her head was bobbing. Dude knew he was in trouble. I pretended to straighten the Jello as I peeked over my shoulder.

The lady then reached for the Aunt Jemima pancake mix. "This is the shit right here fool!"

The man stood up with indignation and pointed at the box. "What you want that nappy headed bitch lookin' down on yo ass from da cuberd evry monin' fo?"

Woman: "You got a problem with ma hair nigga!?!"

Man: "No Baby. It ain't that, it jus' dat dem white country folks invented dis shit. Our ancestas was all about dat corn bread. If we eatin' cakes we should be eatein' da real thing."

The woman looked at me, flashed a sweet smile, said "Excuse me Sir" and then glared at her man, "Nigga what some white fool know about cookin' dat some slave bitch ain't already got down pat?"

The man now turns to me and I want to run and hide, but stand like a deer caught in the headlights. "Ma Man, if I could tap into your vast knowledge of eats, ain't it true dat dem otha whiteboys be cookin' dat shit up out in dem hills; dat dem country boys be livin' by da skillet?"

The woman flashed me a look that had a smiling mouth topped by a set of eyes that said 'Don't ruin my argument'.

I put up my hands for peace and began my face-saving speech:

"The funny thing is, except for you two, all of the blacks buy Hungry Jack and all of the whites by Aunt Jemima."

She flashed him a wicked grin of victory as his eyes bugged out at me as if at a gender-traitor, and I continued, "Curiously enough, I am one of those country white boys, or was until a few years ago. I grew up in Western Pennsylvania. Up there, there is a family restaurant that is famous for a pancake that takes up the entire skillet, and is an inch thick."

The man sneered down at her and crooned, "You here that Baby, Western Pennsylvania, fuckin' sled dogs en shit en dey got monsta pancakes?"

She seemed crest fallen, about ready to burst into tears or violence as he reached with an ever widening grin for the Hungry Jack pancake mix, so I had to say something to even it out. "You know, up there all we ever ate on our pancakes was Mrs. Butterworth's pancake syrup."

Seemingly in the clear the man grabbed the Hungry Jack mix and then stepped over to the syrup bottle of the portly lady with an apron with a conciliatory smile and said, "Here you go Baby, en you know this old girl is a sista!"

She smiled at me as he pranced, and I could not help myself, and went into my suggestive sales handbook, "And don't forget the Land-of-Lakes butter Sir."

He then, forgetting that his wife was before him, barely having conceded the argument, burst out, "Oh yeah, that fine bitch always in my butta dish."

And then it came, the slap she had been itching to dish out all morning.

Off they went, both smiling at me like I was a family counselor who had saved their marriage.

Now, three decades later, all of these icons have lost their groove except for the sex symbol on the butter box: Hungry Jack's rural white image has been completely deleted; Aunt Jemima is now a middleclass sister dependent on hundreds of dollars of hair relaxer per month, and Mrs. Butterworth has lost her curves that marked her as a middle-aged black woman, now looking like a shapeless android instead.

Only my girl on the butter remains true, dressed in buckskin finery, on her knees.

What might save her from the feminists?

Here is my one hope, and it is born of an inaccuracy in her portrayal, the two feathers in her hair. This was a male warrior tradition, indicating that the warrior had scalped or counted coup on that number of warriors. So, when the PC Nazis come for the Native American Butter Babe, perhaps the fact that her corporate sponsor has credited her with the slaying of two men, might save her for posterity.

One can only hope.

A Reader Response
Akira   July 27, 2014 9:53 PM EDT

Hungry Jack is what I ate growing up (black) in VA. It just tasted better than Aunt Jemima. There was no Mrs. Butterworth syrup on our table. It was Log Cabin syrup. Plus it just makes sense that a Hungry Jack would live in a Log Cabin. The Mrs. Butterworth syrup commercials were creepy and you couldn't really make out her face, for obvious reasons. My household soon moved on to Bisquick, then other fancy pancake and waffle mixes. The same happen with syrup. We looked for real maple syrup at specialty stores. As for Land-of-Lakes, I never paid attention to her. We started to use this brand after my mother got off her margarine kick. Maybe if she looked like the St. Pauli Girl I might have paid more attention.

The Most Dangerous Food: The Ghetto Grocer #10

© 2014 James LaFond

Last night I pulled the dairy order out of the cooler to sort it in the stockroom before putting the sorted goods under refrigeration again. You always want to avoid heat shock, especially with ready to eat products, which is almost every dairy item. It is also crucial to avoid cross contamination. This process should begin with the manufacturer and continue with the wholesaler—but not last night.

Of the two pallets the first one had light coffee creamers and long neck plastic bottles crushed under the weight of butter and carton-packed juice. That is normal, about $100 down the trash chute every night before I even get this stuff sorted.

The other pallet really gave me pause. Most clerks just rip out the case cutter and slice open the plastic wrapper, hoping the pallet does not disintegrate into a 1 ton jinga stack. That is why us few clerks who retain better than 50% of our at-birth cerebral function and are not prone to show up drunk or stoned for work, are detailed to perishable duty by the one dude in the joint who can actually spell and sign his own name. [He wears a tie if you happen to be looking for him.] If I had cut the wrap and the shroud underneath, we would have lost half of the $2,000 yogurt order from cross contamination. That is the best case scenario.

The worst case scenario is I'm on vacation and Mush Mouth Mike cuts the shroud and all two gallons of bacteria laden chicken blood drain through the unsealed cases of yogurt and cottage cheese, and then gets on the clerk's hands as he puts up your ready to eats, and clings to your granny's Activia yogurt cups, and people start dropping their bowels on kitchen and dining room floors all through the neighborhood—and the dude in the tie who can spell is not a happy camper and Mush Mouth Mike spends the rest of his life as the janitor in the nastiest ghetto store in the chain.

Those five heavy blood-dripping cases of raw chicken that had been heaved on top of the pallet, and which crushed another $100 worth of yogurt, should not have been so placed. Only the random fact that plastic shrouds are placed over freight selected in one department before the order picker cruises to the other department saved this order. The raw chicken would be placed overtop of ready to eat lunchmeat without a shroud, that is why it should always go on the bottom. But always and never are not applicable when it comes to safe food handling among our degenerating work force.

Back in the day we had a chicken cooler in which large wax-coated cardboard cases of raw chicken were stored and the low man on the meat room totem pole chopped it up. Those coolers smelled so bad that I have seen men pass out upon entering. I once saw 7 construction workers drop like flies in October when they tore down a chicken box during a summer remodel.

A USDA inspector once told me that two thirds of all chicken that passes inspection is diseased and that the meat cutters and cooks should handle the nasty bird corpses as if it were toxic waste. For that reason chicken has been cut at plants and shipped out ready packed for the last decade.

The chicken is the food animal most likely to make you shit your guts out and is the leading candidate for generating a pandemic of avian flu, probably in southern China. If you must partake of this nasty beast here are some shopping tips.

Never Buy

1. Chicken that is not displayed in a factory sealed package with a printed date. If it has been wrapped in the store and dated with a scale-generated price sticker than the seal was busted or it is outdated chicken that has been rewrapped by the likes of Rancid Ray, legendary slum meat cutter of Northeast Baltimore.

2. Chicken that has spices sprinkled on it in the package. This is done to cover age-discolored meat.

3. Chicken that is leaking blood from the package. Remember chickens are the Eboli sufferers of the farm animal world.

4. Vegetables 'for grilling' that have been displayed in the chicken section or any part of the fresh meat case. Even if cross contamination does not happen in the display case, the veggies have been trimmed with a meat knife that may very well have been used to gut an out of date chicken package.

5. Cheese that is displayed in the fresh meat case. This is explicitly against Health Department Regulations in Maryland, but is a common retail reality.

6. When you get this dirty bird home treat it like a recent victim of a zombie attack and decontaminate the prep area with a bathroom grade cleaner.

Bon appetite!

'The Candy Man Can': But Not for Forever: A Ghetto Grocer War Story

© 2014 James LaFond

The Mac Daddy called me today from his post at the largest ghetto supermarket in Maryland. This store reopened 10 years ago after being closed for a decade, and was only able to do so because the company and the municipal authorities made a deal to employ 'overtime' police officers as security, alongside uniformed security and store detectives.

The store manager had noted that with the advent of cooler weather the candy section was missing $600 to $800 a week in shelf stock not accounted for through register receipts. It typically takes 10 days to note such patterns.

As Los Prevention began investigating this, Secci, the non foods manager, noticed a young man in his mid 20s walking toward the front door with bulging clothes. She tapped the man on his shoulder and he ran, giant chocolate bars and family sized bags of candy spilling from his pants and sleeves.

The manager now had the time and the description he needed. These thieves generally keep a schedule as they usually work on foot and travel by bus, to time-sensitive sales locations. Most steal in the evening and resell before midnight at bars. I am guessing this guy hit major transfer points and sold 'office candy' to employees headed to work in their corporate cubicles.

Video research pinned the Candy Man, as he was now known among the staff, down to the half hour preceding 8 a.m. It is 8:28 as I write. The Mac Daddy called me at 8:07 and regaled me with this tale as the Candy Man was being taken out to the paddy wagon. The company will prosecute.

Usually shoplifters are not prosecuted, simply being fined the cost of the goods they attempted to steal plus $50. With this video evidence the retailer is hoping to get this guy convicted on a felony. When I worked for this company 10 years ago Baltimore City police would not arrest a shoplifter who had less than $300 of goods on them or had damaged an equal amount in their bid for freedom. Since 2009 and the economic dip and attendant higher drug addiction rates shoplifters—particularly those who back talk responding cops or are brazen enough to steal from under the nose of an off duty cop working in a security role—are shown slim mercy.

The problem is there may be no room for this guy in prison and he is probably an addict and will return to his trade as soon as released.

'The Crazy First': The Ghetto Grocer on the First Day of the Welfare Month

© 2014 James LaFond

Yesterday Miss Ezz called me with a trifling tale of ebonic workplace transgender politics, wanting to unload a bit of her insanity over the phone, then cut herself short, "I'd really like to get this off of my chest, but what can I say Baby Cakes, it's *The Crazy First* and here comes another retarded bitch looking to shovel a load of shit that this girl is not about—later!"

That truncated call to The Land of the Relatively Sane from the mad house that is urban retail food got me thinking that I've been focusing too much on 'foodstampers' and their EBT accounts that load up in alphabetical order like monthly lottery windfalls and power up the retail food economy between the 6th and the 16th of each godless month of the subsidized year.

On the 1st Social Security accounts become recharged like the life bubbles of video game characters. In the old days this meant that The 1st was senior citizen shopping day. These days retail food still receives an infusion of elderly money between the 1st and the 5th. But the old folks on social security are now slightly less than half of the beneficiaries of what has become known as The Crazy First.

Miss Ezz called me back to complain about the large numbers of 'mentally ill lazy bitches' who bring their SSI money and 'hormonal tudes' to her establishment on the 1st. I have to agree, and was reminded of one ghetto store I worked at where 5 of the 25 female staffers were out on sick leave, receiving sick pay and prescription drugs for depression as they filed for permanent disability. Between obesity disabled and chemically disabled welfare recipients some stores now seem like mental health facilities on the 1st. Last night, upon reporting to work at Free Food For Fat F...s I decided to take notes and count the overnight SSI customers.

1. 5 elderly individuals, 2 black, 3 white

2. 2 elderly couples, 1 black and 1 white

3. 1 married pair of white chemically disabled 30-somethings, with the male of the pair wearing a red shirt that proclaimed that he was 'ROLLING STONED!'

4. 1 fat tattooed white skank with her Rastafarian sperm donator who were both stoned out of their mind

5. 1 elderly insane white homosexual midget with a pompadour and his 20-something leisure-suited black gay loverboy, these bizarre flamers are monthly regulars

6. 2 mentally disabled people, 1 white, 1 black, attended by their caretakers who seemed to be professional caregivers

7. 2 mentally disabled seniors aided by their adult children, 1 black, 1 white

8. A mated pair of white junkies spending her grandmother's SSI on doughnuts, or what was left of it after they got high and drunk

9. A white stoner skank spending her mother's SSI money on snacks for her black boyfriend

10. The pair of white veteran methhead bachelors who live in a shack full of cats showed up for their monthly supply of canned cat food

11. 3 large, stupid good-natured whiteboys shopping for Granny with her handwritten list. Having no idea what a Cornish hen was they asked me. When I explained about the tiny frozen chickens and where they could be found they looked at me vacantly. Minutes later I went over to the frozen meat section to find them sorting through ducks and turkeys. I selected a twin pack and handed them to the big fat boy who was in charge [these kids were about 15 and this was a school night] whereupon they gazed in horror at what might have been a genetic engineering experiment gone awry. I said, "Nobody under fifty eats these things. They became popular before cheese steaks subs were invented." This seemed to make perfects sense to them, so the leader thanked me as his dumber brothers shook their heads in nebulous cognition, and he marked that particular line on Granny's list with a stroke so bold it seemed to hint that his ordeal was nearly done...

The balance of the customers were weekly regulars and one time drop ins. This is in a quiet suburban location. In busier urban locations like Fort Hood

The Ghetto Grocer

Rat which services a neighborhood overflowing with halfway houses for addicts, convicts and sex criminals, and the abortion clinics that have become 'community centers' who have turned to treating the legions of insane adults generated by rampant drug use, it gets a good deal crazier.

If you find yourself short of money on your next anniversary take the wife to a ghetto supermarket on the first of any month and enjoy the comedy of dysgenic errors that is The Crazy First.

The Nastiest Money: A Tale of Ghetto Grocer Woe

© 2014 James LaFond

This past Saturday morning I received a call from Miss Ezz:

"Do you have a minute?"

"Good, I just have to tell someone who cares—and you care because it will get you a story—about what a crappy day I'm having.

"I come into work this morning and all of the tills are piled up in the cash room. On top of the top till, is a plastic shopping bag wrapped in a paper towel. Stuck to the paper towel is a post-it note which has scrawled in magic marker, 'poopy money' 'handle with gloves.'"

"Yes with a Y. These girls can't put two vowels together unless they're trying to figure out how to misspell their newborn baby's name!"

"I almost punched out and went home. I've never done that, never been tempted in forty years in retail food."

"I peeked into the bag. There is a hundred dollar bill and a twenty. They are crinkled up, like it was sweat pants pocket money. There is a lot of drug money in this neighborhood, lots of cash before and after stamps and EBT cash hit. You can see the smeared shit on the bills through the bag. You can smell it from three feet away."

"At first I was really upset that this cashier accepted money in this condition. Then it occurred to me that the customer most likely did not say, 'Here, I just wiped my ass with this so you might want to wear gloves!' They probably found out the hard way. Ooo this makes you so mad.

"I asked the assistant manager what he thought and he just walked away—another man with no balls, incapable of making a decision. His Boss is on vacation and he certainly is not going to accept any shit rolling up hill.

"Here is the plan. I have gloves and tweezers. But even if I can get it flattened out I cannot run this through the Cashnet machine. I will place this money in an envelope, place that in a zip lock back, put that in a cash pouch, and attach a note for the bank indicating that there is fecal contaminated money within."

I got off the bus after Miss Ezz returned to her grim duties and hit the ATM machine. One of the twenties had been half-soaked in blood, which had thankfully dried, which made me think of Miss Ezz. I stepped away from the ATM and called her voice mail to leave a bloody money message. Then I heard a squeal as the steel-framed glass door began to fall on a lady customer after slipping its pins. I held the door until another man and I could get one pin back in. the woman managing the bank then placed a very large 'Do Not Use' sign on the door with an arrow pointing to the twin door. I said, "Miss, I managed a supermarket in this town for four years. And I have to tell you, that based on the local functional literacy rate, only one in three customers will take heed of the sign."

She looked at me somewhat taken aback, and then rushed inside to get a chair to use as a barricade. One thing you can say about the ghetto is that there are few uneventful days.

The Meat Man: All About Buying Steak in Dark Alley's and Dingy Barrooms

© 2014 James LaFond

Saturday Afternoon: 4:15

After 18 hours walking, bussing, working, training and watching fight films with a sparring partner I decided to stop at the Mixed Race Sports Bar for a beer. By the time the foaming mug was adding another coat of yeasty varnish to the bar top three men came in with two cases of meet: beef and pork. The leader was fifty and wore a culinary jacket as his two apprentices headed to the back of the bar with the 160 pounds of animal flesh.

This man extolled the freshness of his product attested by the bloody aprons of his helpers, who were opening up the folding table that ghetto bars keep on hand so that our hard working black market grocers might hawk their wares. These guys brought knives, butcher paper, and generic shopping bags so I could not determine what outfit they worked for.

They were sold out in 12 minutes, and out the door.

Sunday Night: 7:10

I was walking up a back alley behind the main drag, about to cut through my favorite 2 foot wide alley to the store fronts, when I noticed a lot of activity behind the dumpster. Two men had pulled a 1981 Buick up behind the dumpster and opened the trunk and the two rear doors.

One man minded the mobile store while the other knocked on the backdoors of the eating and drinking establishments. Within the time it took me to skulk 100 feet a crowd of people were picking through the trunk full of frozen fish and shrimp and the back seat full of frozen chicken. I decided to take a short cut through the back door of the lower end bar past the pool tables and to the bar where I ordered a draft.

Just as I relaxed and the happy customers started filing in the back door with arm loads of frozen seafood and poultry, a man with a backpack and a bomber jacket walked in the front door; a tall well-built and handsome man in his early 30s. He was selling two inch thick Delmonico steaks for $5.

The Ghetto Grocer

Tuesday at Dusk

As the rain came down I ran into a lady friend I used to work with outside of a supermarket in the county and we repaired to the drinking establishment in the same strip mall, right on the city/county line. As soon as we got settled and ordered a glass of Forget What I Do for a Living, Otis, the towering dirt-bag bar grocer who used to stand across the street from the store I managed and send crack heads in three and four at a time to overwhelm my security, walked in.

Now Otis is working the county, sending female heroin addicts into Walmart and higher end supermarkets on raids. In fact he proudly carries his T-bone steaks and fillet minion into the bar in a Walmart insulated bag. He was selling $15.99 packs of steaks for $5. One pass around the bar and another back and his bag was empty and his wallet flush. As he crossed the sidewalk he threw the Walmart bag in the trashcan and went about his parasitic business.

The one thing all of these criminal meat venders have in common is they move their product so fast it does not even get warm; their need for speed and their customers' need to feed combining in the best interest of product freshness.

www.ingramcontent.com/pod-product-compliance
Lightning Source LLC
Chambersburg PA
CBHW050437290526
45786CB00006B/2058